PERMISSION TO DIE

CANDID CONVERSATIONS ABOUT DEATH AND DYING

Eric Kramer, M.D.

Kellie L. Kintz, M.S.W., L.C.S.W.

Stuart Bagatell, M.D.

Rabbi Anthony Fratello, M.A.H.L.

PERMISSION TO DIE
CANDID CONVERSATIONS ABOUT DEATH AND DYING

 **SEAK Publishing**

seakpublishing@gmail.com

All photographs were taken at Woodlawn Cemetery, West Palm Beach, Florida

Acknowledgements:

Special thanks to the City of West Palm Beach for permission to photograph Woodlawn Cemetery, a historic cemetery developed by Henry Flagler in 1904.

The original iron entrance gate was removed in 1925 and replaced with a concrete arch on which the inscription from the original gate—"That which is so universal as death must be a blessing"—was recreated. The origin of that inscription remains a mystery.

Photography Credits:

Lois Spatz
loisspatz.com

Cover and book design:

Jay R. Pizer
www.imaxproductions.com

Printed in the United States of America

Publisher's Cataloging-in-Publication data:
Kramer, Eric
Kintz, Kellie L.
Bagatell, Stuart
Fratello, Anthony
Permission to Die / Eric Kramer, Kellie L. Kintz, Stuart Bagatell & Anthony Fratello

ISBN 978-0-692-92421-1

First Edition

DEDICATIONS

ERIC KRAMER

I am thankful for having shared the experience of the miracle of life with my wife and children —and all of the souls who have graced my travels. Merrily, merrily, merrily, merrily life is but a dream.

KELLIE L. KINTZ

To Tom, Caitlin & Megan: God gave me you, and you have shown me what it means to be unconditionally loved and undergirded with strength by my faith and my family in both good times and bad. To Dad, Mom & my "extra" parent Stowers, Kimberly & Kevin: together we have experienced the painful death of loved ones, and each in our own way have transformed that pain in to an effort to lighten the burdens of those who suffer. To Jeanne McDonough Southworth, LCSW: As my mentor, you are a shining example of extending compassion and empathy to those in need. You have exemplified grace in the midst of crises.

This book is a tribute to each of you. I love you with all my heart.

STUART BAGATELL

I would like to dedicate this book to the memories I have of all four of my loving grandparents who have taught me the importance of family.

ANTHONY FRATELLO

For Joanna, Samson, and Eli, who have made it all worthwhile.

CONTENTS

FORWARD

ERIC KRAMER

Successful aging must include the consideration of the question of, "When should I die?" As technology fulfills its promise of extending our lives, we're faced with the questions of, "How much is enough of life?", and "How should we face the inescapable reality of our deaths?" The quick and obvious answer is that we all want to live forever. The reality, though, is the length of our lives is becoming less important in this era of disposable and replaceable body parts. It truly is the quality of our lifetime that matters more and more every day.

How does a conversation begin about a topic that we can't talk about—that no one really talks about? Where is the jumping off point to cut through the intellectual definitions and the sterile antiseptic medical terminology to reach a place in which real words, experiences and feelings can be used to speak about the unspeakable? Who has the capability, the depth of experience, the sensitivity, knowledge, or even more, the audacity to give themselves license to discuss our universally shared last act on the planet?

All of our respective cultures acknowledge the magnitude of death as the major event it is with structured behaviors and traditions. Afterlives, reincarnation, heaven and hell are all constructs that may help us deal with the consuming emotions of loss and humanly unanswerable questions surrounding the permanence of our souls. We would like to present for consideration, from a perspective of our own personal experience and that as healthcare workers, the idea that since death is inevitable, reasonable and appropriate we should embrace the concept and give ourselves and our loved ones the opportunity to die in a well-planned, dignified manner.

Without any pomp or ceremony, and with considerable humility, the authors of this volume attempt to advance the conversation that we've all never had about death—not someone else's death—not the stages of dealing with death—not the objective chemical reactions associated with death—and certainly not the legal definitions or issues of outside agencies' involvement in death—but of our own, not to be denied, impending exit from this life.

We, who live with death each day of our professional careers, want to reach and speak out. Beyond our own individual indoctrinations, we, who have seen untold unnecessary suffering of patients and their families, want an opportunity to contribute to changing the conversation from life at all emotional, physical, spiritual and financial costs toward a release from fear and guilt and acceptance and celebration of life's natural conclusion. We offer: *Permission to Die.*

 # INTRODUCTION

STUART BAGATELL

The contents of this offering are the collective stories of a Cold War kid turned Neurologist, an innocent daughter who became a psychotherapist, a Little Leaguer who became a physician, and a grieving grandson who grew up to become a Rabbi. The seed for this book was planted during a hospital ethics committee meeting at an academic community hospital where the four soon to be authors found themselves seated around a table. The clinical ethics consult brought forward to the committee on that day revolved around a common theme; caring for one with a serious and terminal illness. After the obligatory comments about the principles of patient autonomy, patient rights, advance directives, living wills, healthcare surrogates, and code status were made, one individual's voice rang out, "If only the patient had permission to die."

After the meeting, the four of us came together on several occasions over the next few weeks, and agreed upon the need to share our collective experiences with not only other healthcare professionals, but with the population at large. We decided to lay out our thoughts in chapter format, with each chapter consisting of the individual contributions from each author. The order of the entries is as follows: Eric Kramer, Kellie Kintz, Stuart Bagatell, and Anthony Fratello.

First Dance with Death seemed like a good opening chapter to allow the reader to get a sense for the humanity of each of the authors; that we are not pompous professors or egotistical beings, but fellow humans with emotions and feelings regarding death. *First Professional Death* gives the reader a glimpse into our professional training and how those experiences shape our views on death. *A Good Death* is the authors' attempt to describe what they imagine to be a good death but fully admit that it has no clear definition. *Waiting to Die* includes stories about people and their families who are forced to face death. *Death and Grace* is a chapter that each author took the liberty of interpreting in his or her own way, and the product is a wealth of experiences and feelings from those who see death every day.

We hope that you find meaning in this book, and that it comforts you to know that you are not alone as you travel through this world.

1

FIRST DANCE WITH DEATH

ERIC KRAMER

I t may have been as late as when I was fifteen that death became personal to me. I had grown up in a very small and isolated extended family where both of my grandfathers had died at young ages before I could know them. No one in my family was even remotely ill when I was a child. My father, mother, two grandmothers, three brothers and my uncle were my world.

I experienced the magnitude of the country's and world's grief at the Kennedy assassination but didn't feel personal loss at the tragedy. The injustices evoked by the civil rights and anti-Vietnam War movements were news items that captured my attention. In this setting as a confused and depressed teenager, I had read about and even written about death many times. But I was a middle class white kid who didn't go to Vietnam and was spared the pain of knowing anyone who was killed there. I could write all I wanted to but really, maybe luckily, my words were romantic cathartic summaries not of feelings but suppositions.

The closest experience I had regarding death was in reading the book, Death Be Not Proud, which clearly contributed to charting and sculpting my course in life. This biography depicts a young boy's fight against a brain tumor that eventually leads to his demise. Stark, gripping, frightening, sad. Moving in a way that stirs the emotions, but in the end only one's personal reality after experiencing a primal event can sear-in our own manner of feelings.

At fifteen I was at the funeral of my best friend's brother. He had been a beautiful young man who just wasn't able to navigate in what was his tremendously turbulent life. The father, two older brothers and an older sister were very successful both personally and financially. My assumption was that he couldn't find a safe psychological harbor and began exploring destructive behaviors. In the 1970s it was far too easy to embark on a destructive pathway.

At the time of his death his people were known as extremely strong physically and emotionally. Midwesterners after the family had come from Germany, they were an American family reflecting all that that phrase represented in the 1960s. He never gave himself permission to get the type of help he needed. Later it would become evident that there was psychiatric disease in the family

I was close enough to the family that I was asked to be a pall-bearer at the funeral. I didn't think I deserved the honor and was even inwardly embarrassed. Why should I be given such a position if I didn't feel their loss? I didn't know how to feel their loss.

I watched my close friend. I was very close to him through collective coming of age experiences that young boys have while becoming young men. We'd stayed up many nights analyzing and curing the world's ills. We'd thoroughly traded opinions on everything from girls and rock music through politics and religion. We'd competed together in sporting events and occasionally overindulged just a little in celebrations. But I didn't understand his and the family's feelings. I didn't know what to do to help them through their pain – as if there was a prescription. I grieved for them but I couldn't grieve with them. I've never forgiven myself for that personal shortcoming.

KELLIE L. KINTZ

I met Death at 11 years old. It was an unwelcomed first dance. I was in 6th Grade, enjoying my role as my favorite teacher's pet, the music of the late 70's and my friends. In one beat, life was innocent and sheltered and in the next, it was not.

This first dance with death occurred with unparalleled swiftness. My friend Kristi, the funny girl who drew cartoons and made us laugh when we should have been paying attention to Mrs. Erwin's class lesson, had died. She and her brother were riding bikes and playing "chicken." Kristi lost control of her bike, fell, hit her head on the pavement and never regained consciousness. She died days later.

The surreal-ness of her funeral, a memory forever locked in my brain. The church filled with blank faces dressed in seemingly floating cloaks of black. Pain was not abstract that day, and was hanging heavy from the ceiling while forcing itself into the room from the floor. The witnesses to this horror sat still, each stunned in to a dark silence except for the sounds of Kristi's parents' anguished sobs.

My best friends, Cindy and Mary, sitting too far away, their faces mirroring what I was feeling: confusion, panic and fear. At 11 years old I understood that death was permanent, yet I was not capable of wrapping my brain around the reality of this situation.

The full force of the pain of Kristi's death enveloped me when I reached out to Kristi's Mom after the funeral service ended. Kristi's gregarious Mom, who everyone adored, was emotionally gone. The palpable life was literally knocked out of her. In its place remained a vacant stare filled with dark eyes that were scary to peek in to. I remember that gut-wrenching feeling of bile in my throat, and a shiver up my spine.

Fast-forward to Fall, 1978. I was about to meet Death again at age 13. Losing Kristi was painful, yet this second dance with death would become the polarizing moment in my life. It was my life's dialectic: it knocked me off my feet and provided me with the foundation for my life's work.

Let me explain. My Dad, Charles D. "Mike" Talbert, and I ran a few miles together each evening. In the Fall of 1978, those runs became less frequent. A brilliant aeronautical space engineer for NASA and Bendix Avionics, my 34-year-old Dad was in pain, and the cause was undetermined. His 6'4" 210 lb. frame began to change and he was unable to control both his weight loss and loss of strength. The most difficult thing for me to watch, as a 13-year-old, was the obvious pain he was experiencing. He tried to hide it, but I knew. And I'm certain it hurt me almost as much as it hurt him.

Many details from this time-period are clear, and yet, somehow, there are many details that are cloudy. Maybe as a protective mechanism? (I often wonder if memories that are too emotionally dark are clouded for us because we are not supposed to remember.) Due to this memory-haze, parts of the overall story leading up to this point don't make sense when I re-tell it, so you must forgive me.

I remember feeling that I was too cool to Trick or Treat that Halloween, my Dad's 34th birthday. I chose to stay in my bedroom upstairs watching scary movies on the Creature Feature Channel. My Dad took my younger sister Kimberly and younger brother Kevin trick or treating, and it was obvious he was in pain. I remember being alone in my room, steadfastly praying, asking God to help him to be pain free. That prayer haunts me to this day. I know it shouldn't, but think about it for a minute and you'll see why it does.

I am unable to recall the details of Thanksgiving that year (I do remember a For Sale sign in our front yard, but the memory is fuzzy, especially since we didn't move), but memories of Christmas are eerily clear. My Dad had lost a significant amount of weight and was in constant pain. His face was drawn, his blue eyes cloudy. His skin color had a yellowish tint, as did the whites of his eyes. There was a noticeable odor surrounding him, one that words can't describe. (Years later, after working where I've worked, I know that odor all too well). He was very slow and methodical in his physical movements and he spent more time alone in his room. I found the adults whispering head to head in hushed tones around him to be unnerving, especially when they would end their conversations as I walked in. It exacerbated my fear. Little did I know that my second dance with death was beginning in the background.

My Dad spent hours setting up a Christmas gift for me that year. When I opened the gift, a sewing machine, he smiled a soft, tired smile, the light in his deep blue eyes dim.

I was moved to make extra efforts in wrapping his gifts that year, decorating the outside of his packages with the cartoons that he had patiently shown me how to draw as a child. Is it possible that on some level I knew death was near and I was holding on to what would too soon be gone?

After New Year's Day, my Dad traveled with my Mom's parents from Brandon to their home in the city of Atlantis, for what we were told would be a time of rest and relaxation. What they did not share were the medical evaluations he was scheduled to undergo at JFK Medical Center. Over the course of those few days, darkness enveloped our home. We were existing but not living. My sister's 10th birthday went unnoticed. Within days, unexpectedly, my grandparents returned to our home in Brandon. My Dad was lying wide-eyed in the back seat of their car, unable to lift himself up.

Sunday, January 14, 1979, my Mom and grandparents were murmuring about a plan to fly my Dad to Duke University by Air Ambulance for medical care. I was in a fog, unable to process what was going on as I paced on the periphery of the chaos. I remember my sister and brother were sent to a neighbor's house. It was as if the three of us were separated by the layers of dense pain that filled our home. We weren't communicating to one another and no one was communicating to us. We were 13, 10 and 7 years old and were in what I imagine now was shock. My memories flashed back to the pain of Kristi's funeral.

I have a vivid memory, unfortunately, of walking in to our kitchen to get a glass of tea that afternoon. My Dad's Mom was on the phone in our kitchen, speaking with a family member. I overheard by Dad's Mom discussing medical care, as well as the phrase "inoperable pancreatic cancer." My Mom was nearby in the laundry room, standing in front of the clothes washer when I crashed in to her after running from my Grandmother's words. My Mom stared at me, both of us in shock, and briefly hugged me before I quickly ran away.

Hours later, my parents called me in to their bedroom. My Dad, sitting in his rocking chair, mustering the strength to smile, joked with me and made me laugh. He was such a funny man, gifted with not only an insanely brilliant intellect but a wicked sense of humor. I'd give anything to remember the words we shared.

Pushing the thoughts of what was happening out there away, I hid within the protective walls of my bedroom, with the wild stripes my Dad had painted on the walls and matching comforter my Mom had gifted me, my own stereo and TV. My room brought me comfort, and allowed me to avoid reality for just a little while longer.

My Dad and I enjoyed watching football together, our favorite team the Dallas Cowboys. He would quiz me on players' names and records, and I loved impressing him with my near photographic memory. He loved that I could throw a spiral pass, and bragged to family and friends that I was a cheerleader with a quarterback's arm. It seemed fitting to distract my mind that night by watching the show, "How to Become a Dallas Cowboys Cheerleader" on TV.

Mid-show, my barrier of protection was eerily broken by a knock at my door. Painfully slowly entering my room, my Mom's Dad, speaking in riddles, leaned towards me and said, "We did everything we could."

A heart beat later, my Mom's Mom joined us and said, "Your Mom needs you now." I was frozen, for a moment.

And then, in a dark black crash of emotions, I understood. The stalactites and stalagmites of pain that filled Kristi's funeral were now present in my room, coming towards me from the ceiling and the floor.

My grandparents were trying to gently tell me, their oldest grandchild, that my Dad had died. In our red brick, two-story home that he had loved, that we had loved, as they prepared to transport him to Duke University for treatment. At age thirty-four, a promising career, married to his college sweetheart with three young children... this dance with death ended, and swept my Dad off his feet.

My first instinct was to run. Literally. I ran aimlessly down the stairs and landed in the living room near my piano. I banged out notes on those black and white keys, surprised that with each note the pain only strengthened. I ran out the front door. I ran around the same streets my Dad and I ran each evening. I ran and ran and ran until I couldn't catch my breath. I was running away from the pain. But it caught me. And it hurt. Bad.

STUART BAGATELL

My dad and I were making the drive from home to my Elementary School's baseball field for Little League practice that Saturday morning back in 1987. It was the summer before 7th grade, the start of my junior high school years. It was a time when the mind and body were constantly playing leapfrog with one another; you wanted to kiss a girl but your voice still sounded like one. Who had time to think about death?

Brian was my friend since pre-school and our families were close friends. Brian was on my baseball team that summer. About a mile from the ball field, a newsman's voice crackled over the radio, "Breaking news here in Farmingdale. A 12-year old boy was killed in a freak accident." Brian was getting ready for a camping trip with his family. Apparently, Brian was leaning into the back trunk of the family Jeep Wagoneer when the rear window began to close. Brian's neck got caught in that window which would not retract. Brian was asphyxiated. Baseball practice was cancelled that day.

I had no idea what to think. I remember feeling scared and shocked. I remember replaying the gruesome scene of Brian's death in my head repeatedly for several months after it occurred. I remember my dad's look of disbelief and the extra tight hug he gave me on the way back to the car from the ball field.

Brian was Jewish, and in accordance with Jewish Law, would be buried the next day. I wasn't going to miss this; I was curious. but I also wanted to say a proper good-bye to my friend. I had never been to a funeral.

Seeing the black casket and the family in tears is a flash in my memory. Standing at the grave site with the hole in the ground, the bright green grass all around, and the casket hovering over its final resting place haunts me to this day, but I'm glad I saw it. When I discussed this memory with my father, he remarked, "I remember you wanting to get as close to the gravesite as possible; we couldn't pull you away." I had nightmares for some time afterward.

My family and I paid a Shiva call one night during the week after Brian's death. I remember hugging Brian's mom, but she was numb from the Valium. Brian's father, older brother and older sister sat dumbfounded. I was in a house of mourning. I observed in uncomfortable silence.

At the start of the new school year, all the recently graduated sixth graders were invited to a tree planting ceremony on the front lawn of the elementary school. The flag was flown at half-mast, and a beautiful stone engraved with Brian's name was set at the foot of the tree.

Thirty years have passed since Brian's death, and I have been fortunate to accomplish many things. In my role as a physician, I have the privilege of helping people and their families cope with the inevitable and every time I facilitate an end of life care discussion or bear witness to a patient enduring a fatal illness, I see Brian and his family. But among all the things I have done with my life, I am most proud and overcome with joy when I think about my two sons. I cry as I write these words thinking about ever losing them. Brian's death shaped my life.

ANTHONY FRATELLO

Even these years later, even after all that has happened and all that I have done, I can still remember what the phone sounded like when it rang. The phone has a different sound when it rings with bad news, as it did that April morning in 1985. I did not need my father to come into my room and confirm for me what I already knew to be true; my grandfather had died. Though he survived the heart surgery he underwent a few days prior, he would not live through the recovery. I groggily told my dad that I would stay home from school that day, and I then did the only thing that occurred to me to do, I rolled over and tried to go back to sleep.

My grandfather's death was no small loss; my maternal grandfather was the patriarch of our family. We were not too many in number, and I had another grandfather I knew, but still in all we marched to his drum. It was his rhythm of life that we followed, from Sunday dinners, to holiday celebrations. We ate when he was ready to eat, and if our schedule had to conform to when he had to go to work, so be it. Often, our conversations revolved around what Granddad said, or thought, or did. We knew that if we were eating out, then after dinner we would go for a short walk. We knew if we were at home, then he would go sit in his spot on the couch and doze for a while. I would often sit next to him, and he would twiddle his thumbs, one around the other and then back again to entertain me, or he would ask me to scratch his back. I remember that back now, it was old and pasty and spotted with age. I can remember now that I would occasionally end up with scrapings of skin under my nails from my encounters with it. I hated that as a child, I miss it terribly as an adult.

My grandfather was an outgoing, friendly man, the kind of person who is generally referred to by saying, "Oh, everyone loved him." He was active in his community; he was a Mason, a past president of B'nai Brith, a popular small businessman. It was infrequent that we would go anywhere and not run into one of his friends. Our family history was replete with the stories of his life; which, were more the stuff of family legend than the larger-than-life variety. We all knew about the various businesses he had had back home in Paterson, New Jersey, about his long marriage with my short, soft, round grandmother, and about how he moved out to California with her, and my mother, their only child, in the summer of 1947.

At an age when most people would be longing for retirement, my grandfather was still going strong; in fact, we tended to believe that it was precisely because he had so much going on that he was still so active. In the years following his move to California, he and a partner opened a liquor store in the Belmont Shore Neighborhood, of the city of Long Beach. In time, my grandfather would become the sole proprietor of "Shore Liquors." Though nominally a liquor store, Shore Liquors was in truth an early prototype of the convenience store; one could purchase a wide variety of candy, dairy goods, ice cream, and even some prepared foods, as well as a full selection of cigars, cigarettes, and tobacco products. To this day, the sweet musty smell of un-smoked cigars takes me instantly back.

At different points and for different reasons, at one time or another each of us—my mother and father, my brother, my sister and I—would have our own time working in "The Store." Some of my fondest memories were those precious summer days where ostensibly I went to work, but were more about people watching, having a leisurely lunch with my grandmother, and coming home with a bag full of candy. For my grandfather, however, The Store quite literally was his life. He was up and out every day at 6:30 AM, 365 days a year. When questioned about retiring he would respond, "The day after I retire, is the first day I go volunteer at the hospital." He had a need to keep moving to be out and about among people. And intrinsically, people picked up on that and responded. Everyone knew and respected my grandfather, from my Fifth-Grade teacher, who was a resident of Belmont Shore and frequent customer, to the community at large, which chose my grandfather and grandmother as the Grand Marshals for the first ever Belmont Shore Easter Parade. To one and all he was simply, Uncle Moe.

It was sitting behind the counter at The Store one summer day, perhaps a year before that April morning, that I first consciously thought about what it would be like if my grandfather died. At 13 I certainly understood death; I had understood death from that time I was 3 or 4 and my brother came to explain to me that our dog had died, and that meant we would never see her again. Though death was a concept I understood, it was far away, remote; death was what happened to other people in other families. As I wondered what would happen if Granddad died, I pondered what the community response would be? Would the Governor attend? After all, George Deukmeijian was a friend of my grandfather from his days as a Long Beach Politician. Isn't that what the Governor did, attend funerals of important people? My Granddad was important! What would happen to my grandmother? "Who would care for her without my grandfather," I thought. What would happen to The Store? It was such a popular well-known institution; perhaps they would turn it into a shrine to my grandfather, no less a pillar to the community as to my family. The reality of the event proved to be quite the opposite in just about every way.

The morning he died, when I finally roused myself out of bed and wandered out I discovered that my mother and father had already left, something about having to go to the hospital "to see." Would I have to see? At the time the house seemed so strangely quiet. This in and of itself took some getting used to. Only a month and a half before our family life was all tumult. In March of 1985, I celebrated becoming a Bar Mitzvah, which meant not only preparing me to lead a worship service, but also the large celebration that would follow. For months, our life and our home were filled with hubbub and constant errands and a million little tasks each one of which had to be performed. Both before and after there were comings and goings of family members. And then, there were the minor incidents that indicated clearly that my grandfather did in fact need the surgery that he had managed to put off for so long.

That he had delayed having a surgery, which he desperately needed, was no secret in our family. He had been told years before he would need a new heart valve, but he chose to put it off. This was a conscious decision on his part to not miss the things he most wanted to see; his 50th Wedding Anniversary, my sister's marriage, and both my brother and I becoming Bar Mitzvah. Aside from family, Judaism was next most important in my grandfather's life. His faith was an undeniable part of his very being. As a young man, I may not have understood what Judaism was all about, but I knew it was important to him, and so it was important to our family. Family friends who were at my Bar Mitzvah Service recalled the look my grandfather had when he came down from the Bema following his honor. They said that he looked heavenward, as if to say thank you to God for having witnessed the moment that I became an adult Jew. And then, a scant six weeks later, the operation he had postponed to witness such moments, would take his life.

I remember the funeral. I still recall witnessing how my Grandfather's brothers from the Masonic Lodge gathered in their aprons for their final rites. I can recall how Rabbi Front, with whom my grandfather had an odd kinship, conducted the service. I can remember weeping in the arms of my paternal grandmother as we made our way from the chapel to the gravesite. I remember touching my Grandfather's casket one last time before it was lowered into the ground.

Following the service, everyone gathered back at my parents' home for the traditional Shiva (the Jewish custom of visiting with a bereaved family). I sat for a while on the couch with strange cousins, whom I had never met before, but whose names were frequently mentioned in my presence. I watched as they helped themselves liberally to the food and beverages my parents had provided. I sought refuge for a while in my brother's room, playing the videogames that seemed to bring me more peace and comfort than the vacuous conversation that was taking place in the living room. And then, everything just went back to normal. I returned to school, my parents went back to work, new challenges and new turmoil came into our family life, and we continued on our way. What struck me at the time was not how much things had changed, but perhaps how little. And, as for those things that did change, nothing was the way I anticipated.

The Governor did not attend my grandfather's funeral, and they did not turn The Store into a shrine. My grandmother continued to work long, hard hours in the business, which I realize now was as much hers as it was his. She maintained it for as long as she could, but before too long, The Store, which was in so many ways another actor in our family drama, joined my grandfather in memory.

My grandmother, bereft of both her husband and her livelihood, fell upon her own uncertain path. She had lived so long caring for him and others that without them she seemed woefully out of place. She began a slow decline into infirmity, and to our shame, our family began to look upon her as more of a burden than as the partner of our beloved patriarch. She found peace, and was reunited in death with her beloved in August of 1993, a few weeks before my sister was to remarry.

Not long after my grandfather died, I sat with my mother and I told her about that summer day in The Store, where I daydreamed about his death. At the time, I asked her, "Was it my fault that he died?" She immediately responded, "Put that thought out of your mind." She reassured me that my grandfather died not because of anything I had done, or said, or thought. He died, she told me, because he was old and he was sick and it was his time. As I was to learn later in my own studies, this is not an uncommon question for an adolescent exposed to death at an early age to ask. Psychologists even have a term for this type of question, Magical Thinking, wherein a participant or witness to an event becomes convinced that they are an active agent of that event due to thought or action on their part. I know full well that I had nothing to do with how and why my grandfather died. At the same time, however, I also know that part and parcel of who I am today are precisely because of it.

2
FIRST PROFESSIONAL DEATH

ERIC KRAMER

C rossing through the emergency room seemed like a good idea. I was going to have lunch behind the hospital at a little restaurant and the neighborhood was not one in which anyone took leisurely walks. I wouldn't have to deal with the characters on the street wondering which might harbor ill-will or simply try to rob me and ruin what otherwise would be another controlled fairly predictable day in medical school in 1983. Timing can be everything though. Just as I passed the security desk from the main corridor into the ER I heard, "Code Red Bed 17." I was in my third year of school. I was trained in advanced cardiac life support. I was going to help save a life.

The ER team sprang into action. A lead doctor announced that he was in charge. Nurses materialized from everywhere with various implements, devices and life sustaining elixirs. In an instant, the patient (I realized I didn't even know this unfortunate man's name) was connected to monitors and intravenous catheters. The clinical-technologic ballet that is life saving for so many had begun. Not to be swept aside or miss the event I began chest compressions and breaths as I had been so recently instructed —not thinking about what diseases this person could have had that I was at risk of contracting, because I was a doctor (or soon would be).

What a glorious moment this was to be. For me it was the pinnacle of all that I had ever hoped to do when I first crystallized my vision of going to medical school. For the patient, it would be a grave warning that he had to rehabilitate his lifestyle. I glimpsed a future conversation where we laughed, patted backs and traded our memories – joined together by that decision to take that short cut.

But after the first minutes of the "code" there had been no response of the heart. The monitors were not chirping. It wasn't supposed to happen like this. Then, "All clear", resounded and shocks were administered. Again, no response. I began to look around. The faces of the medical personnel looked grim. I was tiring. More chemicals were given and then more shocks. I noticed that there were no family members or friends peeking through curtains or looking around corners concerned about the well-being of my patient. The team worked on and on. It became clear that it was unlikely that we would be successful. But the team worked on. I fatigued and gave my place to an eager waiting fellow student.

I stepped back. I watched. Directions were being shouted. Hands were busy. I wondered now more about who this person was. I wondered about a life that had led to this moment. I wondered if his significant persons would miss him or if he had any significant people in his life. There was no one there to speak for their friend or husband or son or whomever this man was to someone.

I had a clear realization that this resuscitation would fail. I wanted the emergency room team to share my realization. They kept working. They were working on my friend: The man who was going to help me justify all of the hours and anxiety and fears and self-doubt about why I wanted to be a doctor. And they wouldn't stop. I wanted them to stop. I wanted them to just let him alone now. He was dead. It was OK that he was dead. Wasn't it OK that he was dead? But they wouldn't stop.

I became angry. I didn't know why I was angry. Why was the team, my team not accepting the reality that was so obvious to a third year student? For whom were they working now? To what end? I went out the back door and sat in the restaurant alone.

KELLIE L. KINTZ

The dead give-away (forgive the pun) was the sound of staff whispering. The hissed, low murmurs were an attempt to conceal the drama, hide the pain and protect the living from the knowledge that among them was literally, death. As an undergraduate student completing an internship at both a psychiatric hospital and a nursing home, I stood at a distance, objectively watching these dances as if this were my own laboratory. I marveled at the skill of the clinical staff as they cared for a dying patient and offered support to loved ones close by. I wondered if I would be able to reach beyond myself, putting aside my own painful experiences with death, and provide another human being with caring and compassion.

Would I be able to remain unshaken at the bedside of a dying patient, focusing on the needs of others and not my own? Would I be able to hold the hand of a dying person while still warm or the hand of a dead person when cold, without the loved ones seeing me visibly shiver? Would it be okay if I cried?

It's hard to describe the experience of following the sounds of staff whispering and loved ones crying, knowing you will soon enter into the room of a patient who has died. During the first week of my internship, I found myself walking unconsciously behind a nursing supervisor as she directed me to help her comfort a patient's family who was in distress. The patient had only moments earlier died.

I did not know this patient or his family. I didn't know him as a person, which fortunately (or unfortunately?) allowed for that emotional distance that clinical caregivers often use to mentally compartmentalize the gut-wrenching losses they witness daily. I was acutely aware that this was the first patient I had seen dead. I was also aware that this, this drama playing out before me, wasn't about me. I was mentally shaking myself by the shoulders reminding myself that I must focus on helping the family through the next few hours. I had to, as I had been trained, remain unaffected at the bedside and focus on the needs of others. Not my own.

That, I must share with you, was difficult. This being my first time attending a death professionally—wow, it was very difficult. My exposure to death up to this point was sadly vast, and yet being the caregiver or care-provider on the other side of the crisis was foreign to me. I humbly admit that it took great effort to pull my thoughts away from my own pain and those I knew and loved who had died. My chest tightened as I remembered the deaths of my Dad, my friends Kristi, Gibb, Lauri, David and my Great-Grandparents.

The patient's clinical team members had escorted the grieving family to a more comfortable waiting area to discuss the patient's last moments, with the nursing supervisor directing me to wait in the room for their return. So... the patient and I were alone in his room. Eerily alone. Yes, I had attended open-casket funerals before and seen dead bodies. But, I had never been alone with a dead body and I had certainly never looked closely or even considered touching a dead body. I found myself at once scared and curious.

The patient before me was an elderly man and appeared very thin. I remember thinking to myself that he was "skeleton thin." Noticing that his eyes were not completely closed bothered me, and I wondered if it would have the same unsettling impact on his family members who would be returning to his room very soon. How would the family members who recalled staring in to his eyes over years of a loving relationship cope with the sight before them? The patient's half-closed eyes seemed frightening to me. I stepped in to the corridor and asked a passing nurse for assistance.

I explained to the nurse in the unsophisticated, inexperienced language of a 20 year old student that my goal was to create a lasting picture for this family to view in their minds' eye when reliving this day of loss. A picture that wouldn't haunt them, but would bring peace. Surprisingly willingly, and maybe more to placate me, this kind nurse helped me to dim the lights in the patient's room, to find soothing music to play, to redress the patient in a fresh gown and to reposition him so that his eyes appeared to be closed (even though closing them was, I learned, an impossibility). The scene we set was, in my mind, a peaceful one and I silently prayed as the patient's wife, children and grandchildren entered the room that they were not startled but comforted by the efforts we made. I prayed even harder that I would find the right words to say, and that my words and actions acted as a conduit of God's love for them.

"Peace. It does not mean to be in a place where there is no noise, trouble or hard work. It means to be in the midst of those things and still be calm in your heart. Unknown."

The concept of peace as described in this quote guided me during this first professional experience with death. Where a lack of clinical experience with death and dying caused me angst and fear of the unknown as a student in this situation, focusing on providing peace to this family allowed me to direct my steps assuredly. Because I had personally been there, I had walked those steps to a room to say goodbye to a loved one who had died, I was able to reflect on what would be and would not be comforting. I knew the stuff that nightmares were made of, and I didn't wish this family (or any family) to experience that.

So I comforted them. And gathered all of my strength, breathed in almost holding my breath and said to the patient's wife, "Tell me about your husband." The hour that followed that question being asked was no less than magical. The patient's wife's face softened, and she reached for my hand as she recounted the blessings that the man she loved for almost 50 years had added to her life. Intrigued, and leaning on instinct, basic training and personal experience, I led this wife and family down a lane paved with memories. I found that when I asked the patient's children, "What did you get away with as children that your Father and Mother have no idea about?" the somewhat quiet room erupted into raucous laughter with shared stories of innocently mischievous childhood adventures. This allowed for tangential conversations to build and elevated the expressions of memories in the room to a level that would not have been possible had a) the physical setting of the room not been peacefully comfortable and b) the family not been given permission to show emotion of all colors, and even, yes, laughter.

tion to each limb working proximally to distally. The culmination of the course was marked by the sound of band saws and the smell of burning bone as we removed the top half of our cadaver's calvarium to reveal the essence of life. Our final exam was something out of a budget horror movie; naked corpses positioned on cold metal beds, some prone, some supine, some decapitated with their emotionless hairy head resting comfortably on their chest. Colored pins with tiny numbered flags radiated from the volunteer specimen's various parts. Each pin represented a question that had to be answered in order to get credit.

After spending a majority of the first two years of medical school in the classroom, the third year of medical school was a welcome change. It was during this year that I was exposed to all of the major branches of the field of medicine: obstetrics and gynecology, internal medicine, family medicine, pediatrics, and surgery. During one month that year, I lived in a dormitory situated a stone's throw from a hospital within the "Charity System" of hospitals in the State of Louisiana. This particular hospital was located approximately three hours north of New Orleans, deep in the heart of Central Louisiana. In this part of the country, a pork product is served with every meal, including dessert. Access to tertiary health care services is limited. Learning about obstetrics here would be an amazing experience.

Delivering a baby into the world seemed like a rite of passage, and I was excited to put that feather in my cap. My time would come at 10PM on a Friday night, working alongside a third-year OB/GYN resident; the senior resident was asleep in his bunk down the hall. Surely, people had been delivering babies on their own for thousands of years; no reason to have two physicians oversee the birth of yet another child. In addition, several nurses and assorted medical personnel would be in attendance.

The mother was a 37-year-old, G5P4 at 42 weeks gestational age. That's doctor-speak for a woman who was about to deliver her fifth child and was slightly past her due date. She barely spoke any English and had received no prenatal care with this pregnancy. I gowned, masked and gloved and put some shoe covers over my boat shoes in preparation for what I was told would be a messy endeavor.

My teacher stood by my side coaching me through what he had done hundreds of times during his training. I saw the head crowning, and positioned my hands on either side of the delicate skull, waiting for the forceful ejection of a new life. The big boy came out all at once as I instinctively wrapped him in the warm white towels I had carefully draped over my outstretched arms and cradled him close to my body. I looked in the boy's eyes and waited for the loud cry as I smiled from ear-to-ear. The silence was palpable.

My first observation was the color of the baby's lips and face; he was a pale blue. What seemed like forever but was probably only a few seconds went by without a sound. I was instructed to vigorously rub the bottom of the boy's feet. When this produced no effect, my teacher suddenly turned into a superhero. He quickly made his way over to the warmer and directed me to follow with the boy. I did as I was told, laying the boy on his back under the warm lamps. My teacher listened carefully over each lung field and made mention of the fact that the heart sounds were shifted abnormally away from the usual position. He quickly inserted a plastic tube into the boy's windpipe when it was clear that the boy would not breathe on his own.

I ran down the hallway to get our senior resident, but there was nothing he could do that was not already done. When we returned to the controlled chaos, the radiology team was in place to take an x-ray, and within minutes, a diagnosis of a diaphragmatic hernia was made. This little boy's intestines had found their way from his abdominal cavity into his thoracic cavity, crowding his right lung's proper development, forcing him to face this harsh new environment with only one lung. The feather in my cap would have to wait.

Perhaps a prenatal ultrasound would have detected this anomaly and prompted the mother to deliver the baby at a hospital equipped to manage such a complex birth defect. Instead, the boy I delivered was transported by helicopter back to New Orleans where he "lived" for about a week before he died.

Upon graduation from medical school, I chose to begin a four-year post-graduate training program studying Internal Medicine and Pediatrics. I was fortunate enough to remain in New Orleans for my training, which meant that I would join the ranks of physicians who came before me and would be able to call Charity Hospital in New Orleans, "The place I learned to become a physician." What an honor it was to work at a world renown hospital where over the front entrance, etched in stone, are the words, "Where the unusual happens, and miracles occur."

"Intern on the ramp", shouted the charge resident overseeing our shift in the Major Emergency Room at Charity Hospital. It was night-time, and I was working my fifth night in a row. I was getting used to the change in my normal schedule and was getting comfortable making diagnoses and offering treatments. But I was not ready for this.

The charge resident spoke to a group of interns assembled at the ambulance entrance to the emergency department and said, "When we call for an intern on the ramp, one of you has to greet the hearse outside. In the trunk will be a body of a person who was found dead in the community. You are to perform a death examination and document that you heard no heart tones or breath sounds and felt no spontaneous circulation. Any questions?"

At first, the immature teenager inside of me couldn't wait to get a glance at a freshly dead body. Although I never joined a fraternity in college, I imagined this was what hazing was all about. I was the "Ramp Tramp" on two occasions during my intern year, and each time, I took my job seriously while the hearse driver casually smoked his cigarette waiting for me to complete my task.

Room Four in Charity Hospital's emergency department was the stuff of legends. It was here that the trauma victim was resuscitated. On any given twelve-hour shift, there could be as many as fifteen "room four activations." Gunshot victims, victims from motor vehicle collisions, stabbing victims, and victims of domestic violence would be ferried in by ambulance. As the intern in room four, it was my job to insert a plastic catheter into the patient's bladder while the team examined the patient. When it was time to flip the patient onto his or her stomach to complete the examination, it was my job to perform a rectal exam to ensure that there were no signs of traumatic spinal cord injury or gastrointestinal hemorrhage.

A 25-year-old African American man who had sustained a gunshot wound to the head was wheeled into room four at 2AM on a Saturday night. As we took our positions, the charge resident at the head of the bed instructed everyone to stop what they were doing. After unraveling the gauze that was haphazardly wrapped around the patient's head by the local first responder, the resident noted the unmistakable sight of brain matter gushing from a gaping hole in the back of the man's skull. His pupils were fixed and dilated. He was unresponsive. Correction, he was dead.

As a pediatric intern, I worked for a few months on the oncology ward in our children's hospital. A 15 year old-boy named Brett was admitted to the hospital for his first of what would be several rounds of chemotherapy. He was diagnosed with an aggressive osteosarcoma after a bone in his leg failed to heal after a traumatic injury. Brett was an avid baseball fan, and was a child of divorce. Brett's illness brought his parents together, if only during the times he was hospitalized.

I worked with Brett each time he came in for treatment. He endured awful pain, gut wrenching nausea, and losing his hair. After months of treatment, Brett's tumor was not yielding. Later that year, Brett's leg was amputated. No more baseball; no more riding his all-terrain vehicle. He could still fish.

After completing my residency training, a couple of years after Brett lost his leg, I ran into Brett's mom, Susie, at a local grocery store. We had not seen each other for quite some time. I was bleary eyed from staying up all night with my newborn infant and was waiting in line to pick up a few items. Our eyes met, and Susie said, "Don't I know you?"

"You absolutely do", I said without hesitation. "How is your son?"

Susie seemed reassured. "That's right. You used to play Nintendo games with him when he was in the hospital. He liked you. Actually, Brett died last month."

Our conversation played out in front of Jane, the woman who had rung up my groceries several times in the past, as she completed Susie's transaction. I offered my condolences to Susie but felt uncomfortable under those circumstances. I was quite surprised yet comforted by her words, "Brett is safe now and he is no longer in pain. God will take care of him." I usually made small chit chat with Jane after I shopped, but the conversation today was short and to the point. Jane summed up it nicely, "That was beautiful."

I graduated from residency training in the aftermath of Hurricane Katrina. Immediately after the storm, few children remained in town, so the bulk of my training occurred in the tertiary care setting caring for deathly ill kids. During my time in the pediatric intensive care unit, I experienced the death of a two-year-old boy and witnessed the reaction of the boy's mother and father. They were so crippled and distraught, that both of them needed to be ushered to the emergency department for sedative medication. It was at that moment that I made the conscious decision to give up on my training in pediatrics and pursue a career in Internal Medicine.

Responsibilities increase with experience, and as a newly minted Diplomat of the American Board of Internal Medicine and as an Assistant Professor of Medicine, I was given the responsibility of taking call at a local nursing home. One Saturday morning, I made my rounds on the sweet old folks who I had come to love and admire. We had received a new admission that morning, so I wanted to be sure that our new resident, Ms. Willow, would settle in nicely to start the weekend. When I visited with the patient and her family, I came to learn that Ms. Willow was in a significant amount of pain. She had just been discharged from the hospital, but was writhing in pain. When I examined her, it was clear that her pain was worsened when I moved her left leg, particularly her hip area.

The patient could not tell me what was wrong, and the family did not seem to know the reason for her pain. I noted in the chart and confirmed with the family that this patient wished for comfort measures only and did not want to be resuscitated if this became necessary. My differential diagnosis for her pain included a fracture, a blood clot, or a simple muscle strain. The first two diagnoses would have necessitated a return to the hospital, as we did not have imaging capabilities at our facility. Since the patient was just discharged from the hospital, I thought it was reasonable to treat the woman's pain and follow up before I left for the day. Since it was the weekend, we needed to open the emergency medicine kit reserved for these types of "pain" emergencies. I ordered the nurse to provide some oral morphine, and asked her to check vital signs every hour until I reexamined the patient.

Two hours went by, and I was preparing to leave for the day. My last stop would be with Ms. Willow. I went into her room that she shared with four other residents. Her bed was in the far right corner of the room. She was laying completely still, her eyes barely open. The morphine seemed to be the right choice.

"Ms. Willow", I whispered. No answer. "Ms. Willow", I said in a normal voice while gently nudging the patient with my fingertips. No answer.

"Ms. Willow", I shouted, while performing a sternal rub (rubbing a closed fist with force up and down a patient's chest bone). No answer. I went out into the hallway and called for some help. Ms. Willow's nurse returned along with a certified nurse assistant as I was performing my physical exam. The patient was unresponsive, was not breathing, and had no pulse. Her pupils were fixed and dilated. Ms. Willow was dead. I cried for 10 minutes alone with the thought that I had killed Ms. Willow. Although I had done nothing "wrong", I was sick to my stomach for weeks, replaying the memories of that early afternoon over and over again in my mind.

These collective experiences have occurred over the course of the last two decades, and I can recall them each as if they had happened yesterday. Death haunts me every day, both inside and out of the hospital, but I have learned to dwell in the happier moments; my son calling my name, my wife giving me a tight hug, a phone call from my mom, a day of golfing with my brother. If death is (like one of my professors used to say) "autosomal dominant with 100% penetrance", then perhaps as a physician it should be my charge to learn the skills necessary to orchestrate a "good death." A good death? What is that?

Anthony Fratello

Throughout its 15-year broadcast run, I was dedicated to the Television Series ER. In an effort to rationalize what was essentially an indulgent pastime, I concluded that it was not the drama of the cast members and plot situations that attracted me, but rather the hospital environment. As a future clergy person I knew that I would spend a great deal of time in hospitals. And thus this TV show provided a view into that cloistered world, it was a limitless opportunity to pick up bits and pieces of practical knowledge, which I could then make use of.

One character that I especially connected with was a young doctor, who had just embarked on his career in medicine. Week after week viewers saw how he struggled with an oppressive schedule and a seemingly insurmountable body of knowledge that he would have to master to be an expert at his craft. I felt that his experiences neatly paralleled my own while I went through Rabbinical School. I also identified with some of the philosophical issues related to his education. In order for him to learn how to deal with people who had suffered horrific health crises, people would need to suffer horrific health crises. What a tremendous irony to a physician's training; to wait for something terrible to happen to someone so that one could then learn how to treat them following their misfortune. I saw myself in this.

I knew all too well, that part of my work would involve dealing with those who had died and their families. To do that, I would have to work with those who lost their loved ones. As a person of faith I certainly did not want people to suffer, but at the same time, the only way I was going to learn how to deal with suffering was for people to suffer. The sad fact was, if I was going to learn how to conduct a funeral, how to perform an unveiling (a ceremonial dedication of a headstone), or how to comfort a family in mourning, then someone somewhere was going to have to die.

Fortunately, the seminary that I attended, the Hebrew Union College - Jewish Institute of Religion, did not leave my hospital and chaplaincy training solely to television shows. Like most of my classmates, during my Fourth Year, I enrolled in a program of Clinical Pastoral Education (CPE). This program is designed to educate clerical students, or anyone interested in a career in chaplaincy, just what that job entails. By immersing students in a hospital environment, as well as providing ample opportunity for personal and professional reflection, the CPE Program gives students the training and education necessary to effectively provide pastoral care to any and all of those who are in need. While the old aphorism that states, "You cannot teach bedside manner," may very well be true in a conventional sense, at the same time one can certainly learn what to do and what not to do at times of crisis.

To complete the 100 hours required to earn one credit of CPE, a candidate had to fulfill both clinical and supervisory elements of the program. My supervisory component consisted of classroom education in conjunction with other students as well as one-on-one sessions with my supervisor. To fulfill the clinical component, in part, I worked four shifts as the on-call chaplain at an area hospital. The job of the on-call chaplain was not only to be available to patients who requested the chaplain, but was also to be a member of the 'Code Team.' When someone 'Coded' or went into cardiac arrest, all over the hospital beepers went off. The Code Team responded to wherever they were called and sprang into action. The more I thought about it, the more I knew that somewhere along the line in one of my clinical environments, most likely as the on-call chaplain, I would find myself at the side of someone who was dying, or who had only recently taken their last breath.

The thought of this didn't scare me per se; it was not as if I had never seen a dead body. By the time I was in my Fourth Year of Seminary, three of my four grandparents had died, and I had seen two of them before they were buried, as well as a handful of other relatives. I was not bothered by the prospect of being in the presence of the recently deceased, but rather what the experience of being there, at the moment, in the room, when the person died. The thought of literally witnessing someone's death gave me pause. Would I be able to live up to my professional duties? Would I effectively care for the others in the room who surely needed my input and advice? Would I be able to care for the family, as I am sure they needed? It was in pondering these questions that I reflected again and again on the irony that physicians must instinctively feel; something bad has to happen so I can learn how to handle it when bad things happen.

My CPE Program lasted from September of 1997 through the late spring of 1998, and as the year progressed it looked more and more as if I would complete my year without what seemed to be the ultimate test. I had befriended and counseled many patients in the Bone Marrow Transplant Unit, where I also provided chaplaincy service. Some had thrived in their treatment, and were released to resume their lives. Others succumbed to their illnesses, but never when I was on the unit. I had completed three on-call rotations that were essentially anticlimactic. I spent more time in the overnight on-call room than I did on the floor. Some of my classmates hadn't been more than 15 minutes into their rotation when their beepers went off. In an effort to put a spiritual spin on things, I reasoned that I simply had not merited being present when someone died. I began to wonder if it wouldn't happen before I was finished with my CPE Rotation, which seemed to be an even worse fate. How would I handle myself as a professional encountering death if I had not had first-hand experience?

I was perhaps 2 hours away from the end of my last overnight shift when the beeper went off. It shook me awake, and after a moment of forgetfulness, I remembered where I was and what was happening. I hopped out of bed and did what I had been trained to do; I carefully dressed, grabbed anything I might possibly need, and I used the restroom—we were taught, "Go when you can, you never know when you will have another chance." Having thus seen to my own immediate needs, I promptly headed off to where I had been summoned.

I wandered through unfamiliar hallways, vaguely knowing in which direction I was headed, until I located the particular room that the pager announced. I walked past the 8-10 hospital staff members who arrived long before me, and I very quickly found myself at the bedside of a dying man, a man I had never met, a man I had no connection to whatsoever. I had no particular assigned task, so I stepped to the side to survey the situation, and I very purposefully put on a face of confidence, as if I knew what I was doing. In truth, however, I expected any minute to be challenged as to why I was in the room getting in everyone's way. No challenge ever came, I did not speak to anyone, nor did anyone speak to me, and I was left to wonder what exactly I was doing there. Why the on-call chaplain was part of the Code Team was never explained to me. I had no idea why I was supposed to be there; I was there because someone told me, "When the beeper goes off, you go." It seemed an odd reason to be standing watching someone die.

The most immediate thing I noticed was how utterly mundane the moment was. This was not at all what I had come to expect. Television and movies tend to portray life and death struggles in general, and CPR in particular, as terribly dramatic moments, lots of edgy music and shaky camera work. In the event, however, it was anything but dramatic. A nurse, or a technician of some sort—I never did discover who it was—was on a riser over the patient and rhythmically pumping his chest. As he labored he looked around the room and spoke with the others in attendance. Some joked, some spoke of their weekends that had just concluded. At one point someone offered to wipe the sweat off of the man performing CPR, but this was done casually, as one might offer to a friend who couldn't mop their brow as their hands were filled with groceries. The whole time I stood off to the side merely watching what was taking place.

A few minutes after I arrived, or it may have been an hour for all I knew, the physician who seemed to be in charge ordered a stop. Everyone paused, everyone looked, everyone listened, and waited for some sign from the man who was the center of attention. He gasped once or twice, and his eyes, which I now noticed had been open the whole time, stared sightlessly at the people in the room. The doctor in charge said simply, "Time of death 0630." It was then that the oddest thing yet happened; the 10 people who responded as part of the Code Team, those lifesavers who had been called in the moment of ultimate need, simply walked out of the room. In a few seconds I found myself alone, truly alone, which was a very strange place to be.

At first I was shocked, then I felt embarrassed, finally I was angry. These people who ostensibly were charged with a most important duty, some would argue THE most important duty—the protection and maintenance of life—seemed to have such a cavalier outlook. While they attended to a man who was dying, they spoke of anything and everything but. Was this a joke to them? Did they not care that a man had just died in their presence? I didn't know the man, he could have been anything: a father, a brother, a husband, a lover, a partner, a hero, a scoundrel. Had these people become so inured to their job that they no longer cared that all of that had just come to an end?

As I struggled to process my discomfort, I suddenly became aware that I was no longer alone in the room. Quietly a nurse appeared and began to straighten things up. She turned off the various machines, which had now become woefully superfluous. She cleaned up the detritus of medical labor that had been, in my mind, rather careless-ly tossed to the floor. She then began to remove some of the tubes and wires that now served no purpose from what was once a man no longer in need of them. As she began to gently clean the patient, I did what apparently I was supposed to do; I too walked out of the room.

I didn't get very far. As I walked back up the hallway, I was met by an elderly woman in a robe and nightgown, who had apparently been summoned to the hospital as her husband was dying. Knowing that it was now my job to offer her the words of condolence and explanation that she surely required, I had no idea of what to say. Should I tell her that her husband had breathed out his last in the presence of 10 people, charged with his care, who seemed not to be bothered by the fact that he was dying? Should I tell her that at the end the man who had been her partner in life was alone, with only a frightened and unsure 25-year old Student Rabbi, not even a real Rabbi, to keep him company? As it turned out, I didn't tell her any-thing, I didn't have to. We were quickly met by his nurse, the same woman who had so diligently neatened his room, and prepared him for his last visitor, and she led us both back in.

I stood there mute, embarrassed now at my own lack of words or action, as this kind-hearted dedicated caregiver explained to a newly minted widow how the staff had done everything in their power to care for her 67-year old husband. She said how sorry she was, and how she would do everything in her power to make certain that her husband's remains were appropriately cared for. This woman, now comforted in her loss, headed out to make her own way in a very different world, the nurse went back to care for her other patients, and I, having completed my final overnight on-call rotation, headed back to school for morning classes.

Within a day of this experience, I had already begun to second-guess my initial reaction. I was too quick to condemn what at first glance seemed to be callousness on the part of the healthcare workers. The doctors and nurses who cared for this man, were hardworking and dedicated. I needed no more sign of that than the way in which his nurse lovingly prepared her patient for the last embrace he would have from his wife, and how he was readied for the last journey he would ever take. Moreover, I have seen the same love and dedication of healthcare workers manifested in countless other ways since that morning in the spring of 1998. How, then, might one account for the seeming indifference?

There is a significant reality that those who see loved ones enter medical care must accept, as devoted and committed as healthcare providers are, at the same time they cannot invest themselves too emotionally in the work that they do. To do so, to be fully present in those moments, means to risk not being able to do the very difficult things that their jobs sometime demand. If every physician's patient becomes a cipher for their father/mother/brother/sister/friend there is no reasonable chance that they can do what must be done, or make the difficult decisions that must be made. There is a sure amount of disconnect that must be maintained, or else the pain of continually waging a losing battle leads inexorably to abandonment of the effort.

I, on the other hand, am not burdened by any such constraints. The mandate of my job as a chaplain, as a Rabbi, as a person of faith, is precisely to connect with the reality of loss and death. As much as a physician may be served by detaching from an acknowledgment of the suffering and death of their patients, I can only benefit from it. In point of fact, I am supposed to. That was the realization that I came to. That was my lesson from this experience. And, at the end of the day, that was why it was so essential that the chaplain was part of the Code Team. It was my job to be present in the moment, to feel the emotion of the event, to connect to the reality of what took place in that room. I was the person in the room whose responsibility it was to witness the fact that something sacred had taken place.

That thought might give the reader reason to pause. Sacred? Can a death be considered a sacred event? Absolutely.

As humans, we are accustomed to thinking of the birth of a child as a blessing. In every faith tradition new life is treated as a cause for rejoicing. How often do we refer to childbirth as a "miracle?" Even people of little or no faith may be wont to use this expression. If we argue that life coming into this world is a sacred occurrence, then we should view life leaving this world as no less so. Death is a moment of transcendence, as one takes leave of their existence in the here and now, and begins their existence in eternity, whatever that existence may consist of. Perhaps realization of that fact is a means toward mitigating the pain and sorrow that we feel at loss. Perhaps realization of that fact is comfort to those who have had to endure the passing of a loved one. Certainly it is difficult to see someone you love die, but in witnessing that, you are witnessing one of the most sacred things you will ever encounter. That is a privilege and cannot and should not be underestimated.

I have met many people in my life; from some I have learned much, from all I have learned some. Over time the names and faces of those whom I worked with, those I have celebrated with or sorrowed beside, have merged into a composite whole. To this day, however, I can tell you the name of the man who died in that Ohio hospital so many years ago. I know precious little about him, and yet so much of who I am, what I do, and how I conceive of my role as a clergy person are a direct product of what he taught me. When I lead a congregation in worship, when I conduct a life cycle event, when I participate in yet another endless committee meeting, I do so because of him. My authority as a rabbi does not stem from the education that I received, the ordination that I bear, or the power that is vested in me by my congregation or the state. My sole efficacy as a clergy person is because I stand there in those moments of Sacred Transcendence. And that makes all the difference.

3

A GOOD
DEATH

ERIC KRAMER

L iving things are programmed to live. Survival is the most basic of our drives. Our instinct to forward the species at all costs was forged on the anvil of unimaginable terror and danger in the jungle or mountainside or desert from which our human ancestors emerged. Life for life's sake is life's legacy.

But we in western industrialized society have altered nature's natural rhythm. Our lifespan of birth, growth, productivity phase and then death, which for thousands of years remained unaltered has been extended and disfigured. When food and shelter were not reliable commodities our time was spent just finding nourishment and safety on a day-to-day basis.

Over time, as our intellect evolved we found that living in organized societies provided for our food and safety needs. Nutrition, sanitation, science and education have promoted the development of the concepts of childhood, free time and retirement. The idea that individuals should pursue their passions and not just material substances to sustain the family arose. There are more of us and many of us are living longer healthier more personally gratifying and rewarding lives. We expect to live pain free endless lives without restriction or limits.

The Buddhist doctrine suggests that, "Life is Pain". And each of our deaths will certainly come. For all of our fancy scientific and religious mumbo jumbo we remain almost embarrassingly unprepared for the one certain passage in our lives. While our science should intellectually prepare us and our religion should spiritually prepare us we remain at a loss. And our deaths should come. We must learn to move over and let the next waves of generations take our place.

In the story of *Little Big Man* the Native American father figure choose a time for his death. "It's a good day to die," he states and goes off into the woods to meet his maker. He was at peace. He had done what he needed to do in his mind. He had lived a "good", just and appropriate life. He had settled the conflicts that he knew of to the best of his abilities. His body wasn't able to answer the promises his mind wanted to make. While he was sad that he would miss his loved ones he felt that his spirit would be free and meet them again some time. He didn't want to be a burden to his family. It was OK to die. He had given himself permission to let go of the pain and angst that living inflicts.

How people face the reality of death will mark our future. Now that we can extend the lifespan to 100 and maybe more, our resources will come more and more into question. How will the planet sustain our growing numbers? How will we live and how will we die? When death becomes a choice rather than a natural inescapable endpoint, who will set the playing field? How will we define the time that we plan our deaths?

And what will we define as a GOOD death? What is a good DEATH? I don't know that there is an answer to either of those questions for anyone other than ourselves. But I believe trying to find the answer starts with consciously accepting the fact and conducting the inner conversation throughout our lives.

KELLIE L. KINTZ

Society on the whole is not ready for open conversations about death. I am reminded of this each time my internal conversation-filter fails me and I mistakenly blurt out seemingly dark words like, "grief work," "death and dying," or "palliative care" when asked how it is that I spend my working hours.

Surprisingly, many in the medical community are not ready to have these open conversations, either. The alteration of our professional language is a clear reflection of this hesitancy to face death as reality. The terms "expired" and "passed away" continue to be used frequently by healthcare workers as they communicate loss to loved ones. The term "death and dying" once used by many medical and hospice workers has been replaced with "end of life care." Political correctness and a desire to soften the emotional discomfort surrounding death are seeping in to our accepted terminology and practice.

Yet compassion for human life should, should it not, encourage us all to advocate for a good and gentle death as an alternative to a medicalized, institutionalized death? And in order to do this, we must, as a society, engage in open (and yes emotionally painful) dialogue about what constitutes a "good death."

Twelve principles of a good death were identified in *The Future of Health and Care of Older People* by the Debate of the Age Health and Care Study Group.

Principles of a Good Death, according to the Debate of the Age Health and Care Study Group, include:

- To know when death is coming and to understand what can be expected

- To be able to retain control of what happens.

- To be afforded dignity and privacy.

- To have control over pain relief and other symptom control.

- To have choice and control over where death occurs, whether at home, in a medical institution or elsewhere.

- To have access to information and expertise of whatever kind is necessary.

- To have access to any spiritual or emotional support required.

- To have access to hospice care in any location, not only in hospital.

- To have control over who is present and who shares the end.

- To be able to issue advance directives, which ensure wishes are respected.

- To have time to say goodbye, and control over other aspects of timing.

- To be able to leave when it is time to go, and not to have life prolonged pointlessly.

Professionally, this list of 12 key and crucial elements is right on target. The "good deaths" I have witnessed have had each of these elements present. Careful review of the 12 principals highlights a common theme: control. A good death, then, affords the dying patient control over the sequences of events leading up to and playing out at the actual event that is their death.

Allowing and even encouraging a patient to take control of their own death demands that we as healthcare workers confront the limits of modern medicine. This is, if we are honest with ourselves, one of the most difficult and emotionally painful tasks we undertake in our professional lives. The curative vs. palliative dilemma churns a storm of internal struggle in the hearts and minds of patients, loved ones and the clinical team. Struggles supported by vast uncertainties surrounding the promises of modern medicine. For every clinical caregiver who has forecasted a patient's imminent death only to have the patient rally, survive and be discharged home to the waiting arms of their loved ones, there are clinical caregivers who have advised life-prolonging and curative procedures only to end in the patient's dependence on chemical or mechanical life support with no hope of meaningful recovery.

Confronting the uncertainties and limitations of the medicalized solutions to poor prognoses demands that we begin to normalize the act of open, clear communication with patients. Admissions of the unknowns, frustrations and fears while humbly sharing that death is on the horizon must become our normal. Granting patients permission to die—allowing patients the control necessary for a good death—begins with this most difficult task.

STUART BAGATELL

When I die, you better second line.
When I die, you better second line.
You better strike up the band, every day of the week,
Parade my soul up and down the street.
When I die, you better second line.

– *Kermit Ruffins, New Orleans Trumpeter*

She had a stroke, but if you are going to have a stroke, this is the one you want to have. What the hell does that mean?

– *Billy Crystal, 700 Sundays*

No one wants any regrets when it comes time to leave the mortal world. I once asked a patient of mine—an elderly man with severe aortic stenosis (narrowing of the main artery leaving the heart) so far advanced that merely getting up from the couch to use the restroom required more energy than his failing heart could sustain—, "What do you think is a good death?" Here are excerpts from his 3 minute soliloquy:

When you're ready! You know you don't want to go to the next step. You don't want to hang around, be a "hanger on"... I enjoyed so much life with my wife Rachel... A heart attack, while you are sleeping... because I'm a coward, I want the easy way out... go to sleep and never wake up. I don't really have a choice... I don't have any choices... I'm tired, I'm in love...".

My parents are in their 70's. At a family gathering several years ago, my mom handed me an envelope. "Those are our funeral plans. When we die, you and your brothers won't have to worry about the small details," my mom said casually. But nowhere in the envelope was there a written plan of what the weeks or months leading up to death should be like. There was no advance directive, no living will.

That envelope sits in the top drawer of my desk in my home office, making me face the inevitable every time I look for a pen or a stamp.

Perhaps a good death is a quick and painless death at a ripe old age after seeing children and grandchildren achieve happiness. But if I were to know that death was not far off (and who can ever know?), I would prefer to spend my last few days at a beautiful mansion with a view of the ocean. I would be engulfed by the smell of fragrant flowers and the sound of birds mixed with a beautiful string quartet and a hint of the ocean waves. I would sip a fine wine or a perfectly aged scotch and just be. My closest friends and family members would each have their own room and would spend their days doing what they loved, coming back to the home for meals prepared by the best chefs and served by the friendliest waiters and waitresses. When I took my last breath, my body would be prepared for burial in the Jewish tradition and sealed in a plain pine box. All who were gathered, along with a New Orleans Brass Band playing soulful yet somber music, would parade from the mansion to the closest Jewish Cemetery where a traditional Jewish burial service would take place. Afterward, the band that accompanied us to the cemetery would strike up a more up tempo beat as everyone, including my soul, "second lined" back to the mansion for a celebration of life. If the envelope in my desk contained a similar plan, perhaps I wouldn't feel so saddened every time I stumbled upon it.

When I am caring for patients who are nearing the end of life, I often ask a straightforward question, "What makes life worth living?" For some, it means being able to interact with others in a meaningful way or being able to enjoy a meal or being able to care for one's own daily needs without assistance. For others, it means simply taking a breath and having a heartbeat. My parents have each answered this question for me, but in two strikingly different ways:

"If I can't wipe my own ass, have the decency to let me die," my mom stated clearly.

"You don't come near that plug until I am dead," my dad pronounced emphatically.

If society were to view the act of dying in the same context as other major life events: baby showers, baby namings, birthdays, bar mitzvahs, proms, graduations, and weddings, then perhaps more people would make more elaborate plans for the inevitable rather than hoping for the best. Instead of spending precious weeks or months in the confines of a dreary hospital's intensive care unit or being ferried back and forth to chemotherapy and radiation treatments, people would instead spend their hard earned money and precious remaining time celebrating life rather than trying to cheat death.

In 700 Sundays, a book that made me laugh out loud and cry uncontrollably at the same time, Billy Crystal writes about his life experiences. In one passage, he plays an imaginary game of poker with God after his mother's death. One by one, Billy picks up the cards that were dealt to him, symbolizing major events in his life:

Card #1	"Maybe five foot seven?"
Card #2	"Lose your father when you're fifteen"
Card #3	"Have your mother her entire life"
Card #4	"Marry an incredible woman, have two beautiful daughters, and now your first granddaughter."
Card #5	"Get to do what you've always wanted to since you first made them laugh in the living room."

Billy goes on to write:

I hold the cards in my hand. He stares me down. I look at them one more time, but I don't really have to. "I'm going to stick, and I'm going to raise you everything I have. What do you got?" I stare at him with confidence, waiting for God to make his move. He stares back. I smile. He folds… He can't beat me.

So what is a good death? I have no idea, I have never died before.

ANTHONY FRATELLO

A aron and Martha (not their real names) had been members of my congregation for many years. In the time that I had known them, we had had conversations together about how they were realistic about their mortality and accepted it as a matter of course. Still in all I was very surprised on the day that they summoned me to their home.

I was NOT eager to visit their apartment home; in truth, I anticipated a chastising. They had not been to services as of late, and I, burdened with seeing to the needs of countless other congregants, had kind of let them slip from my mind. When I received Martha's phone call, and her request to come and visit with them at home, I anticipated a barrage of displeasure that I had forgotten them. I was completely unprepared for what Aaron had to say:

"Rabbi, I have decided I am no longer going to take my dialysis treatments."

I am not a physician. That being said, I do have a layman's understanding of dialysis: in those who are sick, the various toxic compounds building up in the bloodstream, which are nominally filtered out by the kidneys, are removed through artificial means. I am also familiar enough with medicine to know that when someone who is in need of dialysis, does not get their dialysis, they fairly quickly decompensate and die. My first question for my congregant was, "Do you know what this means?"

"Yes Rabbi, it means I am going to die." Having said that, Aaron answered my first instinctual question, "Does this person understand what is going on?" It is not common, but it is not unheard of for people to make fatal health care decisions out of either lack of understanding about what it is that they are choosing, or by virtue of depression. My second question, which I supposed I have been conditioned to ask was, "Are you upset or depressed?"

"No, Rabbi," Aaron said with great confidence. "The truth is, that I have been like this long enough, and I am ready." He then proceeded to tell me that he woke up the day before and said it was time. He spent a few minutes convincing his distraught wife that this was the correct course of action to take, he then took time to notify his family, and finally concluded that he had to summon me. It wasn't so much that he wanted my opinion or approval — I don't think he was overly concerned what Judaism had to say on the subject. Aaron was a proud observant Jew, but definitely marched to his own beat. Rather he wanted to talk it over with someone that he knew, and I flatter myself to say, trusted.

Judaism takes an enlightened view of most things having to do with our bodies. There is no strong puritanical narrative in the Jewish experience. Tradition teaches that our corporeal nature is not essentially impure or of less value than our spiritual sides. Judaism does not hold that anything about the body is inherently sinful or corrupting. In point of fact, there is a blessing that is said upon using the restroom that says, in effect, "Thank You God for the fact that my body works the way that you designed it to." Our bodies are as they are and do as they do, as that is how God has determined it should be. Death is no exception. The tremendous irony about death, at least where the Jewish tradition is concerned, is that it is simply another part of life. Whereas we do not welcome it, celebrate it, nor seek it out, we are also not supposed to imbue it with fear and loathing. Jewish Law (Halakhah) is fairly explicit in declaring that whereas we are not permitted to hasten death, we most certainly may remove impediments to dying. It is where we draw that line that most questions come into play.

I gamely explained all of this to my congregant knowing full well that at the end of the day, it did not matter a whit to him; as he was resolutely set on his path. If nothing his wife said mattered, if nothing his family said had dissuaded him; surely my paltry offerings would be of no greater consequence.

I have seen a number of patients who have gone without dialysis, and thus I was fairly sure what would happen over the ensuing hours and days. I felt comfortable enough to share this with Aaron's family. I explained that within a few days of no treatment, toxins would build up in his blood that would begin to affect his mental faculties. The increasingly clouded blood, so to speak, would inexorably lead to an increasingly clouded mind. I warned the family to anticipate this for two reasons. First, I did not want them to be caught off-guard.

Second, I wanted them to know that if they wanted to have their heart to heart conversations, now was the time. I further explained to them that eventually different organs and systems would begin to be affected, falter, and eventually shut down. Death would come perhaps a week later as the body was no longer able to function.

As in so many other circumstances, I was completely wrong, at least where Aaron was concerned. More than a week after his last dialysis treatment he was still going strong. He had gotten a tad weaker, he slept more, and his appetite failed him, but he still had a light in his eyes, a lilt to his voice, and lots of mirth in his heart. His last meaningful conversation with his daughter was filled with the kind of ribald repartee that most of their conversations had been filled with. When he did begin to manifest signs of impending crisis, it was quick and acute. He died suddenly, as if almost to catch everyone who was waiting off guard.

When I have been asked to speak of a "Good Death," it is Aaron's story that I return to. Why? It is simple really. Each of us will die. As sure as we are human we are mortal. There will come a day for each of us when we will draw our last breath, and be gathered to our kin, as the Bible poetically states it. Aaron's death was unique in many ways, however. Most of us labor through life never knowing for certain when we will take our last breath. He did not know for certain when it would be, but Aaron at least had an inkling.

Countless times I have met people who struggle through strained goodbyes as they say, "You never know when it will be your last." In the last weeks of his life, Aaron and his family were not only fully aware of the limited nature of their time, they made the very most of it. Many of us fear dying in a facility or antiseptic environment surrounded by strangers. Aaron died in his own bed, with his wife by his side, after having spent his final weeks in his own space. If this is not the definition of a good death, I am not sure I know what that term means.

Not all of us will be blessed with the prescience that Aaron had. For all too many of us, death will come, again to make use, this time of a Christian Biblical term, "Like a thief in the night." Understanding that puts an extra burden on us as individuals; we should strive not only to live our lives to the fullest, but also to treat others around us with great care and concern. Certainly we all know this, we all have been taught this, and we all intrinsically understand it. And, at the same time, we all forget.

Others of us, like Aaron, will be more immediately aware of our own impending mortality. We may not know for certain when we will die, but we will know the cause of our death. For those who find themselves burdened thus, there are organizations, such as hospice, whose sole purpose is to make dealing with that knowledge more palatable. As incongruous as it may seem, death can be a comforting experience.

4
WAITING
TO DIE

ERIC KRAMER

H e's a beautiful man. I've known him now for over 5 years. I diagnosed him at our initial meeting with dementia. I've observed his slow deterioration from his previously commanding presence to his current state of surrender. In the office today he was calm and resolved. While his wife had accompanied him to the office, I'd learned to see him alone to avoid creating conflicts between them. As is the norm for dementia their reports of his behavior and capacity vary widely. She would be crying – missing and lamenting the soul-mate that she had lost, in the walking and talking body she delivered to these visits. He would chat about anything I brought up in a pleasant manner as if nothing was wrong.

It long ago had become clear that some days were better than others for him. Today was a particularly good day. His content of conversation was full and robust. I asked him about his daytime activities. In a measured tone he replied that he really wasn't doing too much. He told me that he couldn't see too well and needed help to walk. He went on that his daughter had been diagnosed with cancer. And then the floodgates opened up.

"Dr. Kramer, I'm ready to die. It's no big thing really. I've had a good life. I've been very lucky. I have a wonderful wife. But my friends are all gone; I can't see; I can't really do anything. My memory is fading and I'm becoming difficult for my family to care for. My wife loves me. I'm not in pain. Why would I want to go on?"

I was taken off guard. I was thinking in hyper drive. "What do you think happens to us after we die?" I replied. "Do you believe in an afterlife? Do you believe in God?" I was trying to give him time to regroup and let him guide the continuing conversation by throwing out a number of obvious questions. I saw that he was a little uncomfortable that he had confided to me about all of this. He continued in a well thought out response.

"No I don't believe in any God that we have in our Judeo-Christian religious books. I don't believe in an afterlife. I've lived long enough and that's OK with me." He had thought about this before and had cogent answers ready.

I was trying to determine how best to respond. I asked him if he had any thoughts or plans to harm himself. He told me that since he was so dependent on his aide and his wife that even if he did it wouldn't be possible to execute any plan—but no that suicide wasn't an issue for him.

In the end, it was fascinating that we had this discussion in the context of what was supposed to be a routine twenty-minute office visit. It was all very casual and relaxed—almost like discussing his weight or appetite or his choice of a shirt that day. There were no dramatics. He wasn't particularly sad. He needed to talk to someone. In my capacity as one of his long-established caregivers he was comfortable confiding in me. He clearly was resolute, adjusted and comfortable with his conclusions.

I didn't take the interaction any further at that moment. Maybe I should have. I suspended my focus on my schedule and turned the conversation to other topics. We conversed about philosophy and science. We concluded the session with the usual inquiries about sufficient medications and the determination of an interval for his follow-up visit.

Is it possible that for some people it is very reasonable not to value continuing to live? I don't think my patient is wrong – for him. I've known him for years. He never wanted to be incapacitated physically but now is cognitively. I've seen more than several others with various medical conditions who have told me the same. "Frankly, I'm just waiting to die." This isn't even surprising to me anymore.

We as physicians are taught, do no harm. I have been asked to kill a patient once. A family member observed her loved one after a stroke and demanded that I simply increase the sedative until he stopped breathing. I respectfully declined and excused myself from the care of that individual. I will never harm a person who has put their trust in me. But am I harming a person who has calculated that they would prefer dying to continuous daily suffering – even if it not horrible, grotesque suffering. Who am I to require someone continue to live? Does "physician" mean life at all costs or while treating the soul beyond the body can death be a rational reasonable choice?

KELLIE L. KINTZ

I do not remember his name, but I remember his face. Filled with tenderness, his deep brown eyes pulled his caregivers, both family members and clinical team, to him. Unable to speak due a tracheotomy with ventilator dependence, he delivered his clear wishes to us by writing on an ever-present steno pad. The last entry said simply, "I am ready to die."

13 letters. 5 words. 1 powerful meaning. This man…a husband, father, brother, friend who had suffered the ravages of Lou Gehrig's disease, had made a conscious decision to end life-prolonging procedures and to allow the disease process to take his life. He was 49 years old.

His wife, children, parents and siblings were at his bedside in the Intensive Care Unit. All were visibly shaken. Their attempts to remain strong were thwarted by the anticipatory grief that brought them literally to their knees. Their crying was not confined, vacillating between delicate tears and guttural sobs.

The medical doctor on our team wrote the order for removal of life support with tears brimming in her eyes. We stared at one another, silently, as if we knew what the other was thinking. As she discussed the details of the patient's wishes with the clinical team, the patient's nurse excused herself from the room. It's a hard reality but there are times when it's simply impossible to hide as a clinician how difficult it is to consider that a human life …a precious life… will be lost.

No amount of education or training allows you to be prepared for the devastation of such a case. A young man, happily married and blessed with children and a promising career, diagnosed with a terrible disease in literally the prime of his life. Valiant attempts to fight and conquer the symptoms of this debilitating disease failed and after weeks of ventilator dependency and continued physical decline, the patient had had enough. His family members hovered over him, attempting to persuade him to not give up, and to fight harder, while his clinical team stood by his side, ready to follow whatever his wishes were.

This brave young man, was at long last given permission to die. I was blessed to hold his hand and that of his wife, as the family and the clinical team surrounded his bedside, praying, while he took his last breaths. His dance with death that had begun long ago was coming to an end, and his body quickly released his soul. Upon his last exhale, I am almost certain I saw a smile spread across his face.

STUART BAGATELL

On the first day of orientation to medical school, we were all given a book entitled "On Doctoring", a collection of essays, poems, and plays related to the practice of medicine. Years later, I reflect on the experiences I have had watching families and patients prolong death, and I think back to a 1968 play written by Kurt Vonnegut which appeared in this book. The play was entitled "Fortitude". The main character is Sylvia Lovejoy, a bodiless head that sits on a tripod. A black box with flashing lights is situated underneath the head instead of a torso. Two mechanical arms protrude from the box. Attached to the bottom of the box are a number of color coded pipes and wires, all of which penetrate the floor below and enter a large control room filled with "pulsing, writhing, panting machines that perform the various functions of organs of the human body." Dr. Frankenstein monitors and responds to every one of Sylvia's physiologic and emotional needs with the push of a button or the pull of a lever. Unbeknownst to me at the time, I was reading a perfect description of care in a modern intensive care unit.

Fortitude means strength and endurance in a difficult or painful situation. I have seen patients and caregivers alike demonstrate fortitude in the face of illness. One particular case occurred during my residency. I was on overnight call in the ICU when a 78 year old woman was brought to the hospital by her beloved husband. When I was consulted, the patient was non-communicative, had labored breathing, was cold to the touch, and barely had a pulse. We concluded that she was in septic shock, likely from an abdominal infection as she grimaced when her abdomen was examined. I did what I was trained to do: I intubated her, placed a central line and gave intravenous fluids in large volumes, started antibiotics, and moved her from the Emergency Department to the Intensive Care Unit. For two weeks, she showed no signs of being able to wean from the vent. Her husband was ever present. Every day, I discussed the grim prognosis with the husband, a simple Cajun man with an undying love for his wife. "Doc, I know she is still in there. She grasps my hand when I speak to her. Please keep trying." At the end of my 4 week ICU rotation, the patient was still on a ventilator.

Two years after that call night, I found myself working at a local nursing home as an attending physician. I stepped into the elevator to head up to the living quarters. A thin old man with thick glasses stood next to a woman in a wheel chair. We glanced at one another, a hint of recognition in both of our eyes. I completed my work, not thinking too much about my encounter on the elevator. When it was time to leave for the day, I stopped by the cafeteria where all of the nursing home residents congregate for meals. Seated at a table near the window were the same folks I met in the elevator. But this time, I couldn't resist, "I think I know you sir."

"Young man, I will never forget you," the man said.

"Is this your wife?" I asked.

"Pretty amazing, isn't it?"

So many emotions overtook me as a chill went through my soul. Although she was wheelchair bound with limited use of her arms and legs, this same woman who I thought would never survive was able to say hello to me, she was able to eat her meals with some assistance, and most importantly, she was able to recognize her husband and enjoy his company. I was instrumental in preserving life.

Conflict, pain, and suffering occurs in cases where patients and caregivers forget that letting go and choosing not to endure is another acceptable option; allowing for a natural death is normal. Doctors and nurses and other healthcare providers have all seen cases like the one I described above, and it is cases like these that are in the forefront of my mind when I discuss end of life choices with families. I never want to take away hope from a family, particularly in cases where an illness is reversible, no matter how remote the chance of recovery. It is those cases where a patient has a terminal illness or an end-stage condition or is in a persistent vegetative state where giving false hope is both unprofessional and unethical.

When I make a decision to suggest withholding or withdrawing care to a patient or her surrogate, it is done with painstaking attention to all of the issues, almost always in consultation with another physician with specialty training in the disease specific to the case at hand, and with the patient's best interest in mind. I never want to go bed at night knowing that I am causing another human being to suffer; prolonging death by way of intensive care when a condition is irreversible and hopeless is my worst nightmare.

ANTHONY FRATELLO

Found in the Talmud is a discussion of the myriad ways in which a life might be taken from the world. "There are 913 varieties of death in this world," the Rabbis declare. "The worst among them is croup, the easiest the kiss.... Death by a kiss is like drawing a hair out of a saucer of milk."(Berakhot)

Those of us who are not going through the active act of dying ourselves are certainly still caught up in its drama. We see death all around us. Those of us who are destined to care for the dying, those of us who will face this most essential of all of life's events, must bear in mind certain truths.

In earlier times when a doctor or health care practitioner suggested a potentially lifesaving procedure, whether or not to proceed was hardly ever in question. In our current age, however, as the practice of medicine has become even more refined, a new question has presented itself: someone may very well survive a radical procedure, but in a state far from ideal. With the rise in potential of long-term invalidity, or as the newer ethical ideal of "Quality of Life" has become part of our conversation, quick and ready acceptance of any and all available options is no longer the norm. Families must accept the reality that their loved ones may choose to forgo or delay essential treatment that they might otherwise require.

In such situations, it is not uncommon for families to conclude that their loved one is afraid of fighting for their life, or perhaps even out of laziness they do not wish to exert the necessary energy to regain wellness. This is fallacious and shortsighted. Precluding any underlying mental, psychological, or physical issues that may impact such a case, families must accept the responsibility that each of us has to respond to our health care needs as we see fit. More often than not those who make difficult decisions regarding their own care are all too well aware of the implications of the choices they are making.

What is manifestly important for a family to remember is to neither condemn nor condone what someone has chosen regarding their life.

That being said, we must strive to be cognizant of the profound effect a significant loss can have on a family. It ultimately doesn't matter if an individual is well known, or just well loved; every loss has the potential to throw a family into crisis. Moreover, the pain and disorientation a surviving spouse faces is a crucial matter for families and loved ones to be aware of. People often conclude that when a care-receiver is bereft of a loved one, they are worse off than when a caregiver is left surviving. This is not universally the case. To be sure, one who is in need of care and or supervision can suffer with the loss of their partner, but one who has long been in the business of caring for another can be equally traumatized at having the established pattern of their lives entirely undone. In many ways this can be worse, as problems previously minimized now must be confronted, or a life that had been put on hold suddenly has full potential of time, but no sure way of being spent. The only sure thing for a surviving spouse of family member is change. More often than not, that change is not what is expected or anticipated, but of a different quality and nature. Not only must a family or caregiver be able to respond to the loss that someone suffers, but also to the very dynamic and fluid nature of that loss, which can change from day to day or even moment to moment.

I mentioned in the first chapter the notion that had come into my mind regarding my grandfather's passing: had I somehow been complicit in his death because I contemplated it? According to Psychologists, this so-called "Magical Thinking," is quite common. I KNOW full well that I had nothing to do with how and why my grandfather died. At the same time, however, I also know that part and parcel of who I am today are precisely because of it. Is this not too part of a good death? Cannot the impact of a significant loss have a positive effect on the choices that we make? I am certain that my choice of career is largely due to my experiences with my grandfather.

As a youngster my grandfather was Judaism. Though my family was active in our congregation, though I too was being trained in the elements of our faith, the import that it had was still very much predicated on the values that he held so dear. When faced with his loss, the tie that had bound me, so to speak, was severed. In the absence of my grandfather's example, I had to account for my own connection, and thus it was that I began my own Jewish journey. Without his presence to give import to my relationship with God, I had to define my own relationship with God. All faith traditions speak of the importance of honoring those who have passed. Is not incorporating the impact of that passing into our spiritual selves a means toward that end?

When faced with a significant loss, many might have their lives changed for the better. Some grow into a fullness they had not known, or had known differently before the loss of their loved one. The opposite, of course, is unfortunately also sometimes the case. Those who are suddenly cast adrift without that meaning that once had them squared away, never again seem to find a sure anchorage. I have not found any certain way to know who will have which experience. It more often has been the case that those who seemed most able to bear the suffering of significant loss are the ones who crumble. Whereas the others, those whom survivors often worry about, are the ones who rise to the occasion. Still in all, our response to grief is intensely personal and should be treated as such.

A final word must also be said on the disappointments that come with loss. Countless times I have personally witnessed people who were flooded with care and concern upon the death of their loved one, only to be then left alone but days later. It is the shortness of memory, and how quickly things return to normal, that can be the most painful for a loved one to bear. Anyone who deals with loss on a regular or even occasional basis, must be fully aware of the fact that the death of a loved one is not a single moment in time, but a process that can go on for months or even years. To fully and properly manage that loss, one must think not only in the moment, but also keep an eye on the long term as well. It is not always easy to do this when one is themselves caught up in the drama of loss, but is the only way the work of mourning can really be done effectively.

That last aspect of our conversation cannot be emphasized enough. Mourning is work!

We have all encountered countless people who look upon mourning as something of an optional activity. How many times have we heard those seemingly strong, resolute types say, "I won't cry!" The reasons for doing so are varied; anger, misplaced stoicism, an unbound need to remain in control. That being said, we should note that not only is this an impossible act, it is profoundly un-human as well. Many sociologists as well as theologians will agree that the human animal is hardwired to make connections to others. What we must accept is that we are also hardwired to mourn when those connections are severed. To deny mourning, to try to refute it, is a refutation of all we are and all we might hope to be.

As suggested before, there are countless reasons why someone might choose to delay or even avoid their mourning all together. For some this might be a conscious choice, while for others it may well be a subconscious reaction to other causes. The pain of loss and mourning might be so intense, or so intertwined with other life experiences, even ones that occurred in the distant past, the individual is simply unable to face their mourning. Mourning is avoided as an abortive attempt at self-preservation. In the event, however, regardless of whether mourning is avoided consciously or subconsciously, whether it is the result of misplaced stoicism, or deluded self-defense, the end result is the same. Further pain, loss, sorrow.

The need to mourn, as a basic fundamental human drive, means that the pain of loss will find another route to release. Though it might be closed off at one avenue, it will blow at another seam. The impact of delayed or undone morning is immense. I have seen it first hand in my practice. As an individual and a professional, I am convinced that much of the unhealthy behavior we see manifest in society is caused by delayed, incomplete, or undone mourning.

The resolution to all of this, of course, is to very consciously and deliberately perform the act of mourning. We must do the work of mourning. This involves appreciating the significance and impact of the loss. (Ironically, even when a loss is "for the best," the work of mourning must still be done.) This means experiencing and processing the pain that accompanies the loss. It means putting the loss into a final proper perspective, and lastly to recommit oneself to their chosen path in life. Some individuals are able to effectively do the work of mourning on their own. Still others require some assistant to shepherd them through the process. In both cases the goal is the same, to be at peace with the loss, and able to resume the business of life. In other words, A Good Death.

5
DEATH AND GRACE

ERIC KRAMER

1 An 88 year-old woman was admitted to the hospital in an unresponsive state. She had previously clearly told all of her loved ones that, while she really wasn't ready to die, she didn't want any artificial support to prolong her life if a catastrophic even became her. She was though still breathing when she reached the emergency room and the ER staff, despite being informed of the patient's wishes by a daughter, put in a breathing tube. She was punctured for intravenous access in multiple sites. Fluids and antibiotics were given. Still there were no responses though her heart remained beating on its own.

The doctors told the daughter that the patient was alive. They told the family to wait a few days. The doctors said that withdrawing the supportive measures would be the same as killing the woman. In this emergency situation the adult daughter listened to the doctors. If she wanted to respect her mother's declared desires and stop the invasive, heroic treatment she would be a murderer, is what she heard the doctors say. Though her mother had lived a good and long life the doctors didn't say anything about the consequences of the situation and she thought that mom would just get back "on with her life" when she recovered.

For 5 weeks I observed my mother during her vigil at the bedside of her comatose, not quite brain dead mother. Eventually, because there was no hospice at the time, my mother gradually realized the doctors had been wrong. But the hospital wouldn't allow the care to stop. They said she is not brain dead. Eventually I witnessed my mother being forced to choose to withhold feedings from her mother and essentially starve her mother to death. The medical personnel thought they were doing the "right" thing even though they arrogantly ignored my grandmother's explicitly verbalized wishes. I watched and participated as my mother and family suffered immeasurably. Her mother had died on that first day. There may have been some vague traces of electrical discharges in the body lying in the bed labeled with a person's name, but the woman was gone.

The doctors failed my mother and grandmother. They did harm. They enforced their values and beliefs over what made sense. The woman had lived a long and healthy life and accepted death. She specifically did not want what ultimately transpired. The doctors deprived my grandmother of a dignified death. They forced my mother to anguish endlessly and delayed her grieving.

2 In the middle of the night I'm wakened by a call from the emergency room. A woman has had a stroke. It's my responsibility to decide whether she might benefit from a clot-busting drug that might restore her brain circulation. In the hospital 20 minutes later I learn more. The woman is 94 years of age. She recently had surgery. She was receiving blood thinning medications prior to the surgery and had bruises about her body from falls. Most of all I learned that she had severe Alzheimer's disease.

Her family wanted "everything" done. They wanted to preserve the consciousness of the woman who had once been a wife, mother and friend. It didn't matter the expense, which of course was not their burden. It didn't matter that she wasn't aware of the circumstances or who they even were. It didn't matter – nothing mattered – they just wanted to keep the person that they recollected her to be, alive. It didn't matter that that person no longer existed except in body.

3 I work with a 96 year old man. He wants to live. His life has been what most of would consider a living hell, but he wants to live. He grew up in poverty. He went to work before the age of 10. He helped support his family during high school. Afterward, for 8 years, he worked 6 days each week while attending night school to complete his college and graduate education in chemistry. His wife became ill soon after their marriage. He stayed beside her through frequent multiple hospitalizations until her death almost 40 years later. His two sons are compromised and still live with him. He has now been in and out of a hospital 5 times in the last three months. Though he openly regrets any number of events in his life he not only wants to live but also expects to live.

He will though, die. And I will and you will die. But, like wanting to stay up and see the party that the grown-ups are having downstairs, we all want to live just a little longer. Is it that we fear death? Do we know why we want to live? I hear folks say that they want to see a grandchild get married – or they want to reach a certain birthday – but when is it time to die? When is it reasonable to say, "That's enough?" When do we stop torturing a child with cancer, or an older person whose body has just worn out, or some lonely soul in grotesque pain? When is it appropriate and reasonable to accept the reality that we will die? When is life for life's sake inharmonious with being human?

KELLIE L. KINTZ

In her article for Bloomberg Businessweek, "Lessons of a $618,616 Death," Amanda Bennett describes in great detail the sad progression of her husband Terrence's cancer diagnosis, medical treatment, and death. The couple's story and journey through the healthcare system, amassing medical expenses of $618,616 and accumulating 4,750 pages of medical records via care provided by 6 hospitals, four insurers, three oncologists and a surgeon is riveting and awe-inspiring. The question Amanda poses to her readers is thought-provoking: How do you put a price on extending someone's life?

Amanda outlines that two-thirds of the total cost of Terrence's care was for his final 24 months and shares, "the only thing I can see the money bought was confirmation that he was dying."

In my work with patients and families facing end of life decisions, I am often asked, "How do you know what to do? When a physician shares with you that you must choose between curative and palliative care, how do you know which choice is the right choice?" I have, in turn, asked Physician-colleagues the same question. How do you know?

The answer is simply stated yet complex to carry out: Determine the patient's wishes, meet with members of the clinical care team and ensure complete and clear communication, gather all of the facts, request second opinions and consult with specialists as needed, factor in cultural and religious beliefs and norms, weigh the choices and options and discuss openly with family and friends involved.

Unnecessarily prolonging life is an electrically-charged topic. Emotions swing with much volatility as the debate over which life is to be supported is weighed. It is not my intent, nor the intent of my co-authors, to engage in the heated drama of political debate. Rather, to open an intellectual dialogue regarding current society's struggle with confronting death, and granting terminally ill patients permission to die.

The case that rings in my ears as I consider this topic is the case of a young, terminally ill man who had been battling a cancer diagnosis for years. As he lay in his hospital bed, emaciated and weak, dependent on clinical caregivers to provide for even his most basic needs, he reached for my hand and softly whispered, "I am tired. When is it okay to give up?" His wife, present in the room and hearing this, reacted immediately. Raging, she screamed at him, demanding that he maintain a positive attitude and fight for the children. She lectured her husband for 10 minutes on the success rates of the pending treatments he was scheduled to undergo and told him that it was not an option to give up. This man, who had suffered years of painful treatments in an attempt to extend his life, was ready to die. And yet, his family was not able to see this. In hindsight, his clinical team had difficulty understanding this as well. Each physician and nurse responded to his statements of being tired and ready to die with statements of reassurance that the next treatment offered some, albeit limited, hope.

It is quite difficult emotionally to pause and integrate the fact that a younger person who is terminally ill has the right to be given permission to die, too. We as a society are much more willing to allow an older person to stop treatment and to choose hospice ensuring death with dignity when they are terminally ill. Rationalizing this bias in many ways, we encourage life at all costs when it seems to be an unfair pending death...when it doesn't make sense in the scheme of balance in the world. Younger, terminally ill patients make us loosen our grip on fairness. And that, well, that is a shame. Because everyone, young and old, has a right to die a peaceful death with dignity. To those that are terminally ill and able to communicate their wishes, whether verbally or via Advance Directives, they must be granted this permission to die a good death surrounded by who and what they cherish and love.

STUART BAGATELL

F riends of mine who are not Jewish often ask me, "What do you believe happens to someone when they die if you don't believe in heaven and hell." As I walk through the phases of my life, from unencumbered toddlerhood, through elementary, middle, and high school, onto undergraduate studies, my first job as a seventh grade science teacher, onto medical school, post graduate training, and finally settling into a career in academic medicine with the "side job" of being a husband and father of two boys, my answer to that question has morphed into the simple answer I give now: "When you die, you live on in the memory of others."

Shortly before his death from lung cancer at age 40 in September of 1995, Kenneth B. Schwartz, a loving husband and father and successful health care attorney in Boston, established an organization dedicated to strengthening the relationship between patients and caregivers in the changing health care system. Through the work of this organization, the Schwartz Center Rounds were developed.

These Rounds serve the dual purpose of serving as a formal and regular mechanism for caregivers to debrief after experiencing a patient death or dealing with a difficult patient encounter as well as improve patient satisfaction, patient safety, and collaboration across caregiver disciplines.

I never met Kenneth B. Schwartz, but he will live on in the memory of others. Kenneth died gracefully.

Samuel (Simcha, or "joy", was his Hebrew name) Bagatell was born August 2, 1909 in Brooklyn, New York to poor immigrant parents from Eastern Europe. He would go on to marry Gertrude Epstein on January 14, 1939 and have two children, one of whom they named Sheldon on March 14, 1945. Sheldon married Eileen Sitnick on January 28, 1967, and they subsequently had three boys, the last of which they named Stuart Jon Bagatell on February 18, 1975. That's me!

On October 22, 1991, Grandpa Sam and Grandma Gertie were waiting for a bus to take them to Atlantic City, NJ, where they planned to spend the day feeding nickels into various slot machines to pass the time away.

"What time you got, Gert?", inquired Grandpa Sam.

"About 9.", replied Grandma Gertie.

Grandma Gertie retold this story a hundred times in the months to come as these were the last words she heard my grandfather utter. No one knows why, but my grandfather died that day after a long life filled with much joy, a bit of sorrow, and a lot of love and respect from his family.

When my first son was born on January 13, 2009, almost one hundred years after Grandpa Sam was born, I needed to find a name for him. In our tradition, we give our children Hebrew names in addition to their common names. As part of that tradition, the names we choose are usually those of a close family member who has died. Why? So that our children and our children's children will always have a link to their past and remember those who came before them. Those who live good and meaningful lives will be the ones whose names live on and will be remembered for eternity. For my first son, we chose the name Benjamin Sim (short for Simcha, my Grandfather's name). Every time I look at my son or hear his name spoken or see it written on a piece of paper, I am reminded of my beloved Grandpa Sam and all of the memories I had of him for the 16 years I knew him. Grandpa Sam died gracefully.

Harry (Tzvi, or "deer", was his Hebrew name) Sitnick was born on December 10, 1922 in New York, NY to poor immigrant parents from Russia. He would go on to marry Rose Hoffman on November 25, 1944 and have three children, one of whom they named Eileen on May 13, 1946. That's my mom!

When Grandpa Harry (Heshy) was diagnosed with a rare form of bladder cancer, I wrote him a letter (see my entry in the Conclusion chapter). A few years after his diagnosis, on December 5, 2009, he died while in hospice care at the same hospital where I work.

When my second son was born on January 10, 2011, we named him Henry Tzvi. The immense "naches" my Grandma Rose felt when she caught a smile from Henry reinforces that we chose our second born son's name well. Grandpa Hesh died gracefully.

When a figure skater lands a perfect triple axel, we use the word graceful. As we tumble and turn through life, the one thing that is certain is that we will all make contact with the "ice" at some point. How we land is partly determined by how we live. If you want to land gracefully, look to those who you remember fondly, embody their desirable attributes, and pass these along to those you love.

ANTHONY FRATELLO

I remember a man from my congregation. He was a father and a husband. He was a grandfather and a friend. He had worked many years in his home community up North, and he had made his own mark on our community in Florida. Quite unexpectedly, he developed an infection that quickly robbed him of his ability to live on his own. His daughter, understandably, could not be at his side, but I stood with his wife while they disconnected the machines that were keeping him alive. The doctors and nurses told his wife that they were unsure what would happen. Perhaps he might rally and recover. Perhaps he might die. But whatever happened would most likely take time.

When they removed the breathing tube, and turned off the heart pump, he died within moments.

Those who were caring for this man told his wife that this was proof positive that she had done the right thing. "The fact that he went so quickly was a telltale sign that he was really already gone. It was only the machines who kept him alive." The wife walked away from the ICU Room convinced that she had killed the man she loved. This is a pain, which I believe, she harbors to this very day.

There are any number of ways we might approach the question of unnecessarily prolonging life. One might approach the answer from points of view ranging from the suffering of the patient to the suffering of the family. Some in society that are convinced that any mainstream discussion of this subject inexorably leads to the "commercialization" of End of Life Care, as if the timing and inevitability of an individual's passing were to be somehow reduced to crass economics. Anyone who works in a health care environment is absolutely aware of the costly financial considerations that accompany what are ultimately futile medical treatments. At the same time, in my experience I have yet to meet a health care worker who looks at providing care as solely a matter of dollars and cents.

As a religious leader, my approach to this question begins with my understanding of what it is that God wants of us. Here again, of course, there is a lack of clarity. Surely every religious tradition maintains its own standards and thoughts on the subject. Even within Judaism, there is a wide range of belief as to what is and what is not acceptable. (A very fine discussion of this topic from conservative, to moderate, to liberal views can be found in, "Defining Death: The Interaction of Ethics and Halakhah." by Michael Rosen, CCAR Journal, Fall 2006.) Having seen first-hand the impact that unnecessarily life-prolonging measures can have on both patients and families, my own proclivity is to give an answer that combines both facts on the ground as well as with what revealed tradition might dictate.

A Legend: Rabbi Judah the Prince, was one of the most respected of the sages who lived in the 3rd Century of the Common Era. It was he who first took the time to write down and edit what had previously been transmitted only as an Oral Tradition. Thus it was the Mishnah, the authoritative body of Rabbinic Law, was born. The Mishnah in turn is the basis for the Talmud, which is in turn the basis for the rest of Halakhah (Jewish Law). Rabbi Judah was recognized and celebrated as the living embodiment of wisdom and understanding. Thus it was natural that as his death drew near, his students were reluctant to part with him.

They gathered around him and prayed that he should survive. Their prayers kept him alive, though he was in great agony. His handmaid observed his suffering, and ascended to a balcony to beseech God that he should be at peace. When her prayers did not avail, she cast a pitcher down upon the ground. The students' prayers were momentarily interrupted by the crashing noise, and it was at that point, that Rabbi Judah was finally released from the painful burden his body had become. (Ketubbot 103b - 04a)

This is an oft-quoted text that many scholars use to discuss the topic of unnecessarily prolonging life. Again, however, there is no unanimity of its meaning, or what wisdom should be drawn from it. On the one hand, Rabbi Judah's handmaid is praised for her wisdom in knowing what to do to allow his soul to be at peace. On the other hand, a great deal of debate rages on whether or not the intervention of the student's prayers should have been stopped.

From the perspective of those who argue that the handmaiden acted correctly, Jewish Scholars will make reference to another concept in Jewish Law known as the goseis. The goseis is an individual who is very near to death. (A professor of mine once defined the goseis as a person with one foot in the grave and one foot on a banana peel.) Halakhah is clear that in the case of a goseis, we may not do anything to hasten death, but we are permitted to withdraw artificial means of prolonging life.

Whereas it is true that many of the remedies suggested by tradition have been shown by modern science to be of dubious effect it is not the specific action that we should concern ourselves with, but rather the general category. The question that should concern those who head down this path is naturally one that seeks to define the difference between what hastens death and what prolongs life.

From the perspective of those who argue that the handmaiden did not act in accord with what God demands of us, are those who point to the fact that Judaism treats life, indeed all life, as sacred. In multiple places in the Jewish Tradition, we are reminded that only God has the power to decide who shall live and who shall die. Someone who might seek to argue the point would suggest that part of what we have to consider is what is commonly referred to as "Quality of Life." Unfortunately, unlike many other areas where there is in fact a surprising intersection between traditional belief and modern thought, Halakhah does not include the framework for the concept of "Quality of Life." The question that should concern those who head down this path is one that asks, "Are we not already playing God merely by stepping in and prolonging the life of those who should already have passed on?"

As interesting as this ethical discussion may be, what role does it have in the lives of those who are faced with these kinds of difficult decisions? I feel that any family, or any individual who is caught up with this discussion, must ultimately view it through the lens of Three Key Points.

What are the Patient's desires?

One of the few good things that has come out of the very public deaths of Nancy Cruzan, Terry Schiavo, and others like them, is the fact that more and more people have had these discussions. In my own practice, I encourage people to speak about their wishes and desires. Though this is an incredibly difficult and unwelcome topic, individuals must, MUST take the time to make clear to their families exactly what it is that they want. These desires will stem from their own personal feelings; what they have witnessed firsthand, what they have felt, what they have thought, and of course how the values in their lives have impacted their thinking. Second, their decisions will stem from their own thoughts about what is best for their family.

Whenever someone has consciously and clearly expressed their desires, I believe it is incumbent upon those who survive to see to it that those directives are followed. This can also serve to balm some of the attendant guilt that healthcare surrogates frequently feel. Going back to my first story, where the wife in question felt as if she had "killed her husband." In truth, she had done nothing of the kind. She merely carried out what her husband's wishes and desires were. She did not take an active role in his passing, she merely facilitated it.

Where this can become potentially divisive, is when a patient has not clearly expressed their desires and wishes. It is then incumbent upon their family and loved ones to make appropriate decisions. More likely than not, the final decision will fall on one individual's shoulders. Though they will have the ultimate role to play, they MUST strive to consider what every close family member might think or feel. Obviously, the nearing death of a loved one is a time of intense emotional upheaval. Such immense emotions have the very real tendency of exacerbating, or even instigating, what are or have been previously subsumed issues. In these instances, families must put aside whatever they might think or feel and focus on the need to tend directly to their loved one who is in need of care.

Advice of Healthcare Professionals.

Hopefully, in our time of need, we will be blessed to be surrounded with caring and committed healthcare professionals. Whereas it is true that in modern society there seems to be an ongoing reluctance to accept the opinions of professionals, we must recognize that the doctors, nurses, patient advocates, social workers, and others that we meet in hospital settings are trained and committed to their jobs. Moreover, though our experiences are unique to us, they are not categorically unique. Those who are working to care for us have been through what we are going through countless times. We should listen very carefully to the advice, medical and otherwise, that these professionals offer. Even though, it is true, that we frequently will not want to hear what they are saying. The ultimate decisions will rest in our hands, but how we go about making those decisions, should involve the advice of those who are working so hard to care for our loved ones.

Acceptance of limitations.

Modern medicine is a miracle. There are conditions that a generation ago would have killed countless people, which are now thought of as almost as minor issues. What was once a death sentence, can frequently now be reduced to the level of manageable ailment. One need look no further than the fact that there are certain types of cancers nowadays that are classified as chronic. If the advancements that will be made over the next decade continue apace of what the previous have shown, this trend is sure to continue.

At the same time, however, we must accept that there is finality to medical treatment. Even though physicians can do countless things, things that would have been only dreamed of even 5-10 years ago, even they will hit a point at which everything has been exhausted. We must be willing and able to accept that that time, unfortunately, will come. Moreover, we must accept that the practice of medicine is essentially a zero-sum game. No matter what we do for our patients, there is a time and place at which enough is enough. Death is, for lack of a better way of saying it, simply a part of life. No discussion of this topic could leave out a comment about the work of Hospice. Most communities support a hospice center; many have two or three to serve the aging population. For those who are not familiar with the work of hospice, the goal is to care for the patient as they go through their end of life transition. Given that this is something we must all face, it stands to reason that all of us should support the work of hospice.

Contrary to what many think, hospice does not mean, "do not treat." If a patient gets a cold while they are in hospice care, they will be given medication. Similarly, if they have other non-life threatening conditions, they too will be given adequate treatment. What differs between hospice care and traditional medical treatment is that the focus is on palliative measures.

Palliative measures include multiple things. First and foremost, the dignity of the patient will be paramount. Hospice care-workers recognize that though their charges are dying, they are still alive in their care. Second, all reasonable measures will be taken to keep the patient comfortable and calm during all phases of their treatment. It is this facet that makes hospice care so important. I have witnessed firsthand the difference between those who die frequently agonizing or unnecessarily prolonged deaths, versus those who are in hospice care who quite peacefully slip into the next world. Admittedly, there are exceptions to both situations, but the focus of hospice is not on treating illness, but rather helping to ensure comfort.

None of these are easy issues to resolve. Moreover, none are subject to an authoritative pronouncement of what is right and what is wrong. Each of us as potential patients, and as loved ones, has to wrestle with these subjects and come to our own conclusions. That wrestling involves taking countless issues into consideration. To all of those who are struggling with this issue, and even to those who already have a firmly arrived at conclusion, I would encourage pondering this thought, which I always find sobering: Just because science and technology have given us the ability to do something, it does not mean we should do it.

CONCLUSION

ERIC KRAMER

B eyond race, religion, and economics we are all very similar creatures who share defining human commonalities. We instinctually care for our families, fall in love, communicate, compete, and protect and preserve our "selves." We operate on a platform of pre-wired instincts. Cultures in all corners of the earth demonstrate so many similar behaviors that the presence of engrained primitive "drives" simply must be real. What makes us advanced, evolved beings though, is how and when we learn to transcend our reflex reactions, drives or urges and express our individual beliefs and behaviors at a "higher" level.

Our primary instinctual "program" is for self and species preservation. Examples of the inexhaustible energy devoted to preserving life abound at all levels. The value of human life is reflected in our religious cannons and secular laws. Birth, rebirth and even immortality are fundamental themes found in our science texts, liturgies, and mythologies. We lament and mourn those we've lost. We honor our ancestors and construct memorials in their honor. We are willing to undergo even barbaric treatments for the promise of extending life.

We have incredible difficulty discussing or acknowledging that part of life that is our endpoint—death. Perhaps our primal fears require us to suspend our belief that we will die. But death will come to us all. Science in many ways, with our incredible progress and breakthroughs, has made dying harder. And made it harder for our survivors to accept our passing. How we face death, in this moment of fantastic technology and spiritual evolution can be transformed from a primal instinctual abomination toward an accepted graceful passage.

An endless, painless, fulfilling life has become an expectation. Where there is an incurable illness, we doubt and mistrust our doctors. They must be missing something. There must be something they can do. When death is imminent, we wait for a last minute scientific miracle. After all these are reported almost every day.

We each hope to live a long and gratifying life and to die peacefully, painlessly and with dignity and grace. Our instincts though cry, often desperately, for perpetual life. We delay planning for the inevitable. We fear the endless guilt of letting a loved one die without "doing everything." "Life at all costs."

What of, "life for life's sake?" What is the value of life? When the mind has deteriorated beyond recognition, is it "right" to keep a body alive. If the body is unwilling but the mind remains crisp is it humane to condemn a rational person to an unresponsive fleshy prison? Where our blood and spirit, and all that is good, exalt at and maintain the incredible wonder and sanctity of life, it is reasonable that we fear the end of our lives – the unknown of the after death. And for the survivors the primal pain or loneliness at the loss of our earthly connections may conjure the instinctual call for life. But is this a call we should always answer?

What we have seen and learned is that doing "everything" much more often than not accomplishes nothing. There is repeated painful invasion of the sick individual. There is prolonged, often tremendous suffering and pain. And eventually the cycle of sickness and hospitalization for these temporary Band-Aid treatments robs an individual of peace in their last months or days of life. And in the end, we all will die.

The splendor of being human, above our animal brethren, is our ability to choose. We uniquely possess the option to choose our responses beyond our instinctual drives. We can analyze our complex responses to problems and formulate options and solutions that are better than pre-historic animalistic reactions. We can overcome urges or programs that may be counterproductive to mature humane realizations.

Death will never be welcomed. But our collective response to death can mature. Could we learn to greet death as an undesired but expected guest and proceed toward peaceful acceptance? As we've learned and can express humane behaviors such as mercy and charity we can learn to transcend our primitive reactions regarding death.

Not everyone may desire to develop this capability to overcome our fear and denial of dying. But no matter what level of choice of behavior we individually reach, we are all going to die. And no matter what our desires or beliefs we do have a choice in how we face death.

What if it were OK to die? Not that the taking of one's life was acceptable but that there was an honest acceptance of the certainty of dying. Would things really be dramatically different? Funerals and goodbyes would continue. Reflection, respect and remembrance would not diminish. Loss and grieving would occur. We would mourn.

This book is a compilation of the professional experiences of several individuals' interaction with and feelings about death. From the depths of our own instinctual reactions and our various observations we want to reach out. We have personally shared in the loss of family and compassionately seen the suffering of individuals at the altar of technology. We have stood quietly and supportively when there was no hope.

We have wanted to reach out and free people of their anguish. We have each wanted to remove the blame, doubt and the guilt and confusion and to allow grace to take its natural course – to help allow the grieving that must occur and to facilitate the healing that can occur to begin. We have all hoped for and continue to wish to be CARE givers in the most meaningful definition of that term. With this common goal in mind, and by the ability to choose what is right, we suggest a new way of thinking about death and offer, for all of us, the permission to die.

KELLIE L. KINTZ

I am standing at your Mother's bedside in the Intensive Care Unit. My right arm is wrapped around you, holding you close and literally holding you up. My left hand is holding your Mother's hand. This hand is less pink and cooler now than it was when I first arrived. Your Father is pacing in the family waiting room. In his mid-60's, he never imagined he would lose his mate so early, with little warning or time to prepare. My heart breaks for you both as I see the signs of death approaching.

Yes, I understand professional distance and yes, in most instances I am able to maintain this separation between your personal experience and my professional one with you…but…not today. With you, it is different.

You are my contemporary. Like me, you are a woman in your mid-life with a cherished family and a successful career. Unlike me, you have been fortunate to never have experienced the death of a loved one in your lifetime. When we first met upon your Mother's admission to this Intensive Care Unit, I asked you to share with me your experiences with loss and must admit I was caught by surprise at your answer. "None," you said emphatically. "Not a family member, not a pet. None."

A mixed blessing, I thought to myself. A mixed blessing in the sense that not having suffered a loss has protected your heart and mind from the torments of grief, which of course, is a good thing. Yet, conversely, due to this inexperience, you stand with me now paralyzed in fear and unable to imagine how you will cope with the loss of your Mother that is, very sadly, imminent. The doctors have told you that she will not recover and will remain in this state, unable to have a conscious thought or communicate and dependent on machines, and you don't know how you will go on. Compounding your pain is the reality that you, as your parents' only child, never discussed end of life wishes with either of them. Why would you? Death had no grip on your lives and no need for conversation in your homes.

So now here we are, carrying out a bedside vigil surrounded by a machine that hums as it breathes for your Mother, IV poles hung with lines and tubes that provide her with medications that maintain her bodily functions and the knowledge that your Mother is on life-support. You and your Father are struggling with this knowledge.

Your faces pained and anguished, you reach out to the clinical team, pleading with them for direction. Their faces echo your sadness, for they do feel your pain. Doctor after doctor asks you to consider, "What were her wishes? What would she want?" This constant and duplicated query amplifies your pain as you admit between sobs that you just don't know. You never asked.

Reaching out to family and friends, you and your Father ask, "What should we do? Did you ever talk to her about this?"

Personal opinions are given but no one knows what your Mother would truly want. No one discussed it with her.

Family and friends offer differing opinions. A cousin shares via phone that he's seen a recent news report about a woman with a similar illness who was maintained on life support for years while a cure was discovered. A friend demands that you seek second and third medical opinions and keep fighting until you find a cure. An aunt shares that "pulling the plug" is akin to murder and should not even be a consideration. Family members' and friends' personal thoughts tangled with religious undertones and urban medical myths are swirling around you and your Father, causing your thoughts to race out of control.

And my heart continues to break for you and for your Father. But… it breaks especially for your Mother. Oh, how I wish she had completed a Living Will clearly spelling out for you what her wishes would be if she were to face a life limiting illness! The burden and pain this simple document would have saved you and your family is enormous. More importantly, having knowledge of her wishes would have been a gift to you, as you and your Father would have been engaged in a more meaningful bedside vigil as she lay in Inten-

sive Care, rather than being tormented by having to "make the decision for her," as your Father said. "I feel like I am causing her death,"
he sobbed to you. "I don't think she would want to be like this…
in a state of limbo…for any longer than she had to be. The doctors
say there is no hope; she'll always be in that bed and they say she'll
eventually waste away. I can't bear the thought!"

I am sitting with you and your Father now at the foot of your
Mother's bed, and I am silently praying that I find the words to bring
you both comfort.

Your Father quietly cries as I share with him that he is not letting
his wife, the love of his life, down…her body has let her down. His
choices or decisions regarding her end of life care are in no way
the contributing causes of her eventual death. Her illness is, and I
encourage him not to allow his heart to be burdened with this guilt.
I plead with him to listen to my words…I plead with him to acknowledge, when he puts his head on his pillow tonight in what will surely
be a difficult attempt to rest, that he is not deciding death for his
wife should he choose to remove the machines and medications.

I ask you both to share with me your personal thoughts on death.
I encourage you to list in detail what you would want if you were the
patient, and how you would want your family and friends to experience your last days and final hours on this Earth. I ask you to define
what death with dignity means to you.

And as you do, a calmness comes over you both. It is almost as if
you are thinking as one. Your Father gently smiles and wipes your
tears, as he softly says, "My wife, your mother, would not want to
be kept alive artificially. I want her to die peacefully, not fighting
machines." You, in turn, dry your Father's tears as you nod in agree-
ment.

Realizing that the clinical team did everything they could to maintain your Mother's life and yet due to the extent of her illness were
unable to prevent her dependency on life support, you know that
you as a family have truly advocated for your Mother. You did all

you could. You know (and I remind you of this repeatedly during our last hours together) that if the clinical team could do no more, you certainly could not change the course of your Mother's illness.

Facing this pain together, you and your Father speak to the Physicians, and begin the discussion to remove life support. In doing so, you tearfully share with me that you feel that, although you never discussed end of life with your Mother, knowing who she was—you know she wouldn't want to spend her final days bedridden and tied to machines with no hope of recovery. You now firmly offer that this is what your Mother would want: dignity and peace.

As you pray, holding both my hand and your Father's hand, you grant your Mother permission to die.

STUART BAGATELL

Dear Grandpa,

I never thought that I would be in the position of writing you this letter 25 years after taking my first trip to visit you and Grandma at your home in South Florida. It scares me and saddens me to think of you getting older and more frail, but at the same time, I am comforted to know that you are well cared for and much loved.

I hope and pray that you will continue to get stronger and that the years that lie ahead of you are filled with much happiness, little discomfort, and perhaps, another great-grandchild (no news on that front yet, but I will keep you posted).

You have a choice about how you will live the rest of your life, and the decisions made at your appointment with your oncologist this Friday will dictate how you spend at least the next few months. In preparation for you appointment, I have included some questions in this letter that you should think about asking:

1. What is the natural course of my disease if left untreated?

    a. Will it spread and if so, where?

    b. If it spreads, how long will it take to spread?

    c. If it spreads, what kind of symptoms can I expect?

2. What can I expect from treatment?

    a. What are the major side effects?

    b. If I develop the side effects, is there anything that will be done to offset the side effects?

    c. What is the chance that I will be hospitalized again during the course of treatment?

    d. How often do I have to leave my house to get treatment?

e. How long are the treatment sessions?

f. Can family be with me when I undergo treatment?

3. Should I have an advance directive?

4. Should I have a DNR order?

Grandpa, it is very hard for me and I am sure even harder for you to think about dying. But the truth is, as I am sure you are aware, people die. I see it every day. But what most people don't see every day is the way in which people die. More people are dying alone in a hospital, connected to artificial life support, rather than at home surrounded by their loved ones. God forbid your heart was to stop beating properly or you were to have extreme difficulty breathing, doctors and nurses will rush to your aide and perform CPR. This involves forceful compressions on your chest to keep blood pumping to your brain, and the placement of a plastic tube down your windpipe to help provide you with oxygen. You would then be placed on a ventilator and all of your physiologic needs met by a team of doctors and nurses 24 hours per day. Family would have limited visiting privileges, and you would likely be unaware of your surroundings. You could remain in this state indefinitely, and if you don't have an advance directive stating exactly what you would want to have done to you if you were in this state, Grandma would have to make the decisions for you. The chances of a meaningful recovery from most resuscitation attempts are less than 1% (unlike on TV, where most people do quite well after this procedure).

I inform you of this not to scare you or to upset you, or to suggest that this is going to happen to you. I merely want to share with you what I have learned over the last 8 years studying medicine and over the last 33 years as your grandson. When I see death in the hospital, I immediately think of my own family and my own mortality and my own fears about death and dying. I think back to all of the wonderful times I have spent with my family and friends and how much I am loved and I am thankful.

Ideally, we could go back 25 years in time to your kitchen table in South Florida and start over. But we can't. I can't possibly begin to fathom what is going on inside of your head or what your hopes and dreams are at this point in your life, but what I want for you is the rest of your life to be filled with love and wonderful times spent with your family. Whether you choose to undergo radiation and chemo-therapy to fight the cancer or choose not to undergo treatment, I am 100% behind you.

ANTHONY FRATELLO

Tthere is an ongoing joke in my family, it goes like this: When my grandfather was still alive, he led our family Seders (the ritualized Passover Meal). Every year we would comment that the time between when we sat down at the table and the time we actually ate would get shorter every year as he pared down the service. After his death, I took over leading the Seder, and the opposite became the rule: the time between when we sat down and when we ate got longer, as I incorporated more and more traditional elements into our meal.

Though he has been gone for more than 25 years now, I think about my grandfather frequently. We all still tell stories about him, even though our family has changed and grown now to include members he never dreamed of. From time to time we still see people that knew and loved him, though this too is becoming rare as more and more of his friends go their own way. The Store is still there, though many years ago the wall separating it from the barbershop next door was broken down to make a larger retail space. Today it is a boutique offering kitschy items to the new trendy Belmont Shore Community. Belmont Shore has become very tony; there are two Starbucks, but no Shore Liquors. I frequently visit the space The Store once occupied when I am home, and I note the still visible scars on the cement floor from where the cigar case and the walk-in freezer used to be. Even the old floor safe is still there, hidden away under a table of wares, though it has long since rusted into disuse. I am convinced my mother still has a key for it somewhere. For the proprietors and customers of that shop, those worn down marks on the floor represent some of the charm of the space, to me, however, they are and always will be a reminder of what once was. I am also reminded by my son, who was born on what would have been his great-grandfather's 98th birthday.

Were you to ask my colleagues, no doubt they would say the same kinds of things. The dying moments of countless people have touched our lives and tempered our experiences. We are who we are for good or for bad, for better or for worse, in many ways on their account. As we look back on the stories that we have told, we are reminded that no matter how much has happened, how far we have gone, how much has changed, these loved ones are still very alive within. That has been the greatest lesson of all.

When my colleagues and I started writing our stories, we set out to write a book about dying. What it meant to us as individuals and professionals. This was to be a book about what we had learned from our years in hospital rooms, or at bedsides, holding hands with friends and strangers as they took their last breath. It is that, but so much more. We found that this is not just a book about dying, but also one about living. Each of us must understand that dying is just another part of the process, just another part of the ineffable rhythm that all things in life must obey. No matter what perspective we come to the topic from, be it scientific, social, spiritual, or any combination of these or any other human construct, at the end of the day each and every one of us will someday walk the same road that leads to the same end.

What remains for any of us is essentially a choice: whether or not we try to keep the experience at a distance, flee from its contemplation, from its mention, indeed from the very irresolvable challenges that inevitably come in its wake. Or, do we somehow find a way to embrace it? Not celebrate death, not to somehow enshrine it, but to accept it as an inevitable part and parcel of the human experience. Maybe the beginning of that acceptance is in giving our friends, our loved ones, and ultimately even ourselves, permission to die.

REVIEWS

This book is a most important contribution to a question many if not all of us face in the death of those whom we love and care. The authors approach the issues both personally and professionally, a unique approach sharing with us what they experienced and what went through their hearts and souls. Their understanding, lessons derived, emotional reality, religious and medical approaches all add up to the significance of what they are sharing so honestly with us about the death of others as well as our own mortality. Whatever our feelings, predispositions and religious values, these most "human" questions and what the authors have learned and shared warrant full and sensitive thought and discussion. Given as well the realities of modern medical technology, we thank you for your honest and open sharing of your experiences and conclusions.

> – *Rabbi Sheldon Zimmerman, Past President of the Central Conference of American Rabbis*

This book invites us in to a conversation that we may not want to have but need to have. It also brings several important perspectives on death and dying that often do not intersect. As a priest, this book brings both information and inspiration to a subject about which people come to me for counsel all of the time. No matter where you are in life, no matter how close this subject might or might not hit home, this book will help lead to a deeper appreciation and understanding of life and death.

> – *Father James Harlan, Senior Rector, Bethesda-By-The-Sea Episcopal Church, Palm Beach, Florida*

The personal experience of losing a parent at a young age has elevated my sense of compassion for those who suffer. With each family I work with in my professional life who has experienced the death of a loved one, it is my hope that they feel this compassion, and that their feelings and needs are validated. This book provides insights in to how caregivers in the clinical environment validate pain and suffering at the end of life for their patients and their families, as well as validating those of us that are professional caregivers and are exposed to life and death traumas day in and day out. This book has put in to words what I and many of my colleagues experience. I consider *Permission to Die: Candid Conversations About Death and Dying* a valuable contribution to the future education of not only clinical caregivers but funeral directors as well.

   - *Kevin M. Talbert, Owner/Director, Southern Funeral Care- Riverview, Florida*

Permission To Die is a worthy successor to the classic, *On Death and Dying* by Elisabeth Kübler-Ross. I wish I had had this book as we cared for my father in his last days. This is a passage we all make—this book will help you or loved one make the passage with courage and grace.

   - *Joe Tye, CEO and Head Coach, Values Coach Inc., Author, "The Florence Challenge," "All Hands On Deck," " Building A Culture Of Ownership In Healthcare," and "Pickle Pledge."*

This is a very special book. It is written by four individuals— two physicians, a clinical psychotherapist and a Rabbi—who were touched by death in their own unique way. This led to the common realization that dying is inevitable and, while it can be postponed, it is not always right to do so. Treatment can worsen suffering in all its domains—physical, existential and spiritual—without improving quality or helping the patient. They learned that respecting autonomy is more than just asking what one wants, but also explaining what the treatment will do (informed consent) and working with the individual towards a common goal, driven by the results of a thoughtful conversation. They learned that it is OK to allow a patient with an incurable illness to let go; to give them permission to die. Each of the authors reached into their most private spaces and shared deeply personal stories that help bring the message to life.

As a hospice and palliative medicine physician, I found the book a source of reflection and insight. I recommend it, not just to other hospice doctors, but to students, residents and, most importantly, all practicing physicians. Just because we have tools to treat, it doesn't mean we use them or should use them. Giving permission to die is not giving up. It is letting go. We need to learn how to do that. This book helps us put this into perspective.

- *Faustino Gonzalez MD, FACP, FAAHPM, Chief Medical Officer-Hospice, Trustbridge*

The content was extraordinarily honest and very moving. This book offers tremendous insight into both the reality and acceptance of death.

- *Gerardo Aguirre, MD, Medical Director, Medical Care Consortium, Inc.*

I think the book has real potential for discussions that examine end of life issues and medical technology from a variety of points. I celebrate the focus from the clinical to the personal that allows the reader a personal and human insight into four professionals. The book reinforces the sense of the immediacy of time and how, in some cases, it seems suspended. Likewise, the book reinforces the need for open, adult dialogue on what it means to live the last days of life and what choices may be open to people. There are no two "same" journeys even though they all end the same. This book gives a sense of the personal, which to me, is worthy of being stressed. The "process" of death and grief is essentially tied to this.

    – *Rabbi Richard Address, Jewish Sacred Aging Podcast, Director: Jewish Sacred Aging®, LLC*

In *Permission to Die*, the stories these four professionals share are heartfelt and engaging. The concern for their patients is uttermost. Throughout the book the humanity that death and its consequences expose show that even the professionals are profoundly affected by it. I was moved by the compassion of each of the professionals and the vantage point that each brings to the book is fascinating. This book also gives us permission to discuss with our loved ones many thought provoking questions: ideas that death is a sacred event or that we need to be in control so we can experience a good death and how to discuss these ideas with those we love. If science can extend our life or the life of a loved one, is extending life always the right choice? For being a book on the formidable subject of death I found this this book to be very genuine as well as an uplifting read. It lightened my preconceived notions of the burdens and requisites that society seems to place on those dealing with death and its ramifications. *Permission to Die* is a book to be discussed and shared with those most important to us.

    – *Lisa Young Rogers, J.D., Former Assistant State Attorney, Florida*

Unfortunately, we can't all just peacefully go to sleep when we are very old and not wake up. As difficult as it may be, we should talk about end-of-life options. This book will help you get the conversation started, and allow you to see death as just another part of life. I would recommend that first-responders who are regularly confronted with life and death situations read this book.

– *Deborah Fahey, Retired Police Officer, West Palm Beach, Florida Police Department*

The strongest part of this book is the personal stories. Often touching, always honest, moving. This is the biggest difference between this book and so many others out there. The second strongest part is the different viewpoints. The authors represent three disciplines, two of the physicians having differing specialties. I enjoyed this book, especially the personal stories.

– *Kenneth Brummel-Smith, MD, Charlotte Edwards Maguire Professor, Department of Geriatrics, Florida State University College of Medicine*

Sex, politics and religion have long ago been left behind as forbidden topics of conversation but death and dying may represent the last taboo subjects. This book allows the reader to contemplate these topics without fear or loathing but as the inevitable event that it is. It is an absorbing, honest work that provided me with a new understanding and acceptance of my own mortality. Highly recommend for anyone who wants to have a better appreciation for life.

– *Elisa Rodgers, Director of Marketing, Reed Tech*

In *Permission to Die*, two doctors, a clinical psychotherapist, and a rabbi speak in remarkably human voices about their professional and personal encounters with bereavement and mortality. By offering emotionally compelling yet modest testimonies about their attitudes towards and experiences with death, they provide their readers with sensitive guidance about the transience and character of life. The authors share the fears and uncertainties that surround our earthly coil. In so doing, they have written a book of wisdom that is as much about life as it is about death. It is a rare work that informs the minds and touches the souls of its readers as they grapple with the finitude of human existence.

– *Rabbi David Ellenson, Chancellor Emeritus and former President of Hebrew Union College - Jewish Institute of Religion*

In our youth, we think we will live forever. Inevitably, we lose someone and our complacency is shaken. By middle age, the realization we are not immortal begins to creep in. For many experiencing illness or old age, the fear of death hangs like a pall over life. As with most difficult subjects, the only solution is to look the beast square in the eyes. If you're doing this for the first time, however, it might be best to have a guide, to steady your mind, and your heart. The authors face death every day and each, in his or her own way, offers to be your guide. They generously share their personal stories, as well as important events in their professional lives, as they learned to care for the dying. They offer insights and reassurance that a beautiful death is possible. They offer love and guidance. They remind us that death is not the enemy of life. Rather, death is a natural part of life. The enemy is fear. We should grasp the hand of the guide and confront our fear of death, so that, in the time remaining, both we and the ones we love can live our lives to the fullest. Then, when the time has come to die, neither we nor the ones we love will feel the need to ask permission to die.

– *Timothy E. Monaghan, Esq., Partner, Shutts & Bowen LLP, West Palm Beach, Florida*

Since the phrase "nothing is certain but death and taxes, " we seem to be able to give voice in politics to our disdain for taxes while we are silent on the challenges we all face with death...our own or a loved ones. This book gives a voice to a societal challenge—to celebrate death as much as birth. The beginning and ending chapters of our own journeys. Kudos to this writing team for opening the dialogue.

– *Mark Foley, Former United States Congressman*

Very thought provoking, especially for us who have dealt with death so often. I have interacted with thousands of individuals who have had to deal with death. The reaction of many is beyond my scope of understanding. The authors have helped many take a serious look at death and understand it for what it is.

– *Michael Gauger, MSW, Chief Deputy and Senior Executive Staff Officer for the Department of Law Enforcement Operations and Corrections, Palm Beach County Sheriff's Office*

SOURCES

Berger, Thomas. *Little Big Man: A Novel.*
New York: Dial Press. 1964. Print.

Bennett, Amanda. *Lessons of a $618,616 death.*
Bloomberg.com. Bloomberg, 04 Mar 2010. Web.

Crystal, Billy. *700 Sundays.* New York: Warner Books, c2005.
Edition: 1st Edition. Print.

Death of the Age: Health Care Study Group.
The future of health and care of older people: the best is yet to come. London: Age Concern, 1999. Web.

Reynolds, Richard C., and John Stone. *On Doctoring: Stories, Poems, Essays.* New York: Simon & Schuster, 1991. Print.

Ruffins, Kermit. Big Easy: *When I die (you better second line).*
Basin Street Records. 2002. CD.

Smith, Richard. *A good death.* BMJ 320:129-130.
15 January 2000. 8 November 2006. Web.

Vonnegut, Jr., Kurt. *Fortitude.* New York: Dell. 1975. Print.

ADDENDUM

CONTACTS

The authors welcome your feedback and reviews as well as the opportunity to connect with you, their readers. Contact the writing team via:

 Facebook: https://www.facebook.com/SEAKPublishing/

 email: seakpublishing@gmail.com

SEEKING BOOK CLUB FACILITATORS AND ADVISORY BOARD MEMBERS

We, the authors of *Permission To Die: Candid Conversations About Death And Dying*, are seeking selected physicians, nurses, therapists, clergy, first-responders (police/fire), respiratory therapists, hospital staff, nursing home staff, hospice staff, funeral directors & those that have suffered loss in major cities across the U.S. to:

1. Read our book.

2. Share a written "Review" of our book with us via email or Facebook.

3. Volunteer to lead a three-session one-hour "Book Club" in your local area to review the book with others, following our "Book Club Guide." Share feedback from the Book Club with us.

4. Partner with us, as a volunteer member of our Advisory Board, to develop a CEU/CME training program as well as college-level course focused on teaching clinicians how to engage in candid conversations about death and dying as well as how to confront the personal, emotional impact of these losses.

The commitment and gift of your time would be a blessing to our project and would positively impact fellow clinicians and those that face death and dying every day for years to come.

Readers interested in becoming Leaders of our Book Clubs and Members of our Advisory Board may contact us via Facebook at **https://www.facebook.com/SEAKPublishing/** via email at **seakpublishing@gmail.com**.

Very sincerely,

Stuart Bagatell, MD
Kellie L. Kintz, LCSW
Eric Kramer, MD
Anthony Fratello, MAHL

BOOK CLUB GUIDE

Step 1:   Register your Book Club with us via our Facebook page at:
              https://www.facebook.com /SEAKPublishing/

Step 2:   Register your Book Club with a book club website of your
              choice. This will aid in communication with members.
              Suggested sites are: **Bigtent.com; Real Simple's No Ob-
              ligation Book Club; readinggrougguides.com; Ran-
              domhouse.com Reader's Circle; Oprah.com Message
              Boards.** You decide what is best for your Club.

Step 3:   Determine the day, date, time and location for your Book
              Club Meetings. We suggest three sessions, each one-hour
              in duration. You decide what is best for your Club.

The following suggested conversation prompts are intended to help
your Book Club find interesting and insightful ways to discuss, *Permission To Die: Candid Conversations About Death And Dying.*

1. Who are the authors? How do their own circumstances color the
    telling of the story? Do you empathize with them?

2. How did the book affect you? Do these issues in the book affect
    your life?

3. Have you read similar books on the topic of death and dying
    that have provided guidance, support and insight for you? If yes,
    share your experiences.

4. What is the purpose of this book, to teach or to entertain?

5. If the purpose was to teach, did it succeed? Was something
    learned from reading this book?

6. Was there a specific passage of the book that left an impression,
    either good or bad? Share the passage and its effect.

7. Was the purpose of the book to bring light to an issue? If so, did
    it make the group more aware and more knowledgeable?

8. How did earlier opinions on the topic change after reading the book?

9. Was there something especially surprising about the authors' stories? What was it and why?

10. Was there a lesson that can be taken away?

11. The stories are told from different viewpoints. How did this perspective color the story?

12. How do these different perspectives influence your perceptions of the topic?

13. Does the book "break the mold" in any way?

14. This book has been compared to "On Death & Dying" by Elisabeth Kubler Ross, MD. How would you compare the two books?

15. Did you like the book or not? Did you enjoy it? Is it possible to find a book interesting without liking or enjoying it?

16. Has the book changed you? Has it broadened your perspective?

17. Describe your first dance with death.

18. Describe your first professional death.

19. Describe what the authors mean by a "good death." Have you experienced "a good death" personally or professionally? If yes, share your experiences.

20. Share your thoughts and feelings with regard to death and dying and the current landscape. How do your personal and professional experiences as well as your belief systems impact your thoughts and feelings?

21. What do you feel is the most important thing clinicians, first responders and professionals who face death and dying in their work life should remember?

22. If you were to be tasked with teaching young clinicians, first responders and professionals how to deliver bad news, to confront death and dying and to manage the emotions they personally experience in these difficult situations, what would be your top three teaching points?

23. In the professional setting, do you and your colleagues have a specific routine or ritual to honor the dying and the deceased as well as to support the families and loved ones? If yes, please share your experiences.

24. Do you and your colleagues have a system in place to provide one another with support upon the death of a patient? How do you care for yourself after experiencing a loss on the job?

25. Have you shared a candid conversation about death and dying with those closest to you? Are they aware of your thoughts, feelings and beliefs with regard to death and dying? Have you completed written Advance Directives? If yes, please share your experiences. If no, what are you waiting for?

It is our sincerest honor to have you volunteer your time, efforts and experiences to bring attention to the candid conversations we encourage our readers to engage in about death and dying.

We encourage you to share your experiences with us via Facebook **https://www.facebook.com/SEAKPublishing/** or email at **seak-publishing@gmail.com**.

Very sincerely,

Stuart Bagatell, MD
Kellie L. Kintz, LCSW
Eric Kramer, MD
Anthony Fratello, MAHL

SUGGESTED READING LIST

Be Here Now by Ram Das

Dying Well: Peace and Possibilities at the End of Life by Ira Byock, MD

Enjoy Every Sandwich by Lee Lipsenthal

Midwife for Souls by Kathy Kalina

On Death & Dying- What the Dying Have to Teach Doctors, Nurses, Clergy & Their Own Families by Elisabeth Kubler- Ross, MD

The American Way of Death Revisited by Jessica Mitford

The Last Lecture by Randy Pausch

Tuesdays with Morrie by Mitch Albom

When Breath Becomes Air by Paul Kalanithi

CPSIA information can be obtained
at www.ICGtesting.com
Printed in the USA
LVOW03s2033231117
557349LV00007B/336/P